Recovery:
Plain And Simple

Other Books
By
John Lee

The Flying Boy: Healing The Wounded Man
I Don't Want To Be Alone

John Lee
Recovery:
Plain And Simple

Talks On:

Why Men Can't Feel And The Price Women Pay

Saying Good-bye To Mom And Dad

Co-dependency — How To Fight It

What To Do With Your Anger And Grief

Healing Co-dependency And Depression Through
Movement, Sounds And Silence

Written with Bill Stott

Health Communications, Inc.
Deerfield Beach, Florida

The poem by Rumi is from *Open Secret: Versions of Rumi*, translated by John Moyne and Coleman Barks, Threshold Books, Putney, Vermont, 1984, and is used with the kind permission of Mr. Barks.

Library of Congress Cataloging-in-Publication Data

Lee, John H.
    Recovery: Plain And Simple / by John Lee with Bill Stott.
      p.   cm.
    ISBN 1-55874-108-9
    1. Adult children of dysfunctional families — Mental health.
    2. Co-dependents.   3. Men — Psychology.   I. Stott, Bill.   II. Title.
RC455.4.F3L44   1990   90-38579
616.86—dc20   CIP

Publisher: Health Communications, Inc.
           3201 S.W. 15th Street
           Deerfield Beach, Florida 33442-8190

Cover design by Graphic Expressions

For all sorts of reasons this book is dedicated to Frances Lee; Marvin Allen; Allen Maurer; John Hunger; Faith Starnes; Molly Serafin; Rick and Amanda Rose; Betty Sue Flowers; Tom Cable; Jean Barnette; the folks at Listen to Learn; Sheree Scarborough; Mary Jackson; Larry Madison; Roger and Carolyn Fuller; Bill Leland; Ula Zielinska; Marce Lacouture; J.B. Colson; John Duckworth; Karen Luzius; Wayne Kritsberg; Dan Kripke; Beverly Barnes; Charles Whitfield; Chris Brookeman; Dan and Anya Jones; the Thursday CODA Meeting; John Austin; Molly Hocking; Debi and Maya Cope; Bob Abzug; Peter, Gary, Michael, Randy and Marie at HCI; R.J. Kaufmann; Sandra Foster; the Tuesday and Wednesday Men's Groups; Justyna Otowska; Steve Miko; Healing Heart Resources (Chuck and Steven); Anne M. Davis; Tate and Lynda at Kangaroo Productions; Alfred Hornung; Michel Razi; Perry Frank; New Age Bookstore; Bookpeople (Austin); Jim Reeves; Fred Close; Caleb Curren; Gary and Tom and the Dallas Men's Group; the Stotts and the Woodses; and the regulars of the Austin Men's Center.

Our best wishes to all these people — and practically everybody else.

v

Contents

Introduction

Welcome! Come on in and make yourself comfortable. I'm John Lee and you're in the right place. I'm glad you could find the time and the money for some talks on recovery put in plain English and simple terms.

The word "recovery" means different things to each of us. In these talks I tell you what it means to me. I tell you what I've learned in recovery, what I still need to learn, where I hurt, and where I no longer do.

In 1986, at age 34, I finally gave up the most unreasonable of the dreams I had been living for. I admitted I couldn't write a doctoral thesis and so wasn't going to be a college professor. I had been doing part-time counseling for nearly a decade and now turned my full attention to it.

In 1987, after years of false starts, I was finally able to write a book, *The Flying Boy: Healing The Wounded Man,* describing how I had lost my real self as a child and had recently begun finding it.

In 1988 I started giving talks on human dysfunction in Austin, Santa Fe and other cities. This book collects some of these talks.

The talks were recorded and transcribed by Elaine Davenport. They were edited by my friend Bill Stott, whose contribution to the book's form and content is so great that I list him as co-author.

This book is for all of us who want to let go of our parents, our grief, our old loves, our anger and pain, our addictions and dependency. Bill and I hope it helps you in your recovery.

John Lee
Austin, Texas

A Note from Bill Stott

Much of the contents of this book comes from John Lee's lecture series available on cassette tape. Those of you who have heard the tapes will find his talks condensed and rearranged, with new material added from the same talks given on other occasions.

Those of you who have seen John lecture know how he dances about the room, gets his listeners talking and doing, mimics different voices to dramatize different points of view, is sad one moment and hilarious the next. In this book I have presented his talks in a way that gives readers the chance to participate in the excitement of a John Lee lecture with those actually in attendance when he spoke. I have left *you* in the book, you the audience, the seldom silent partner in what John says and thinks. You will see what John does as well as hear what he says. You will hear the audience's reaction and see its influence on him. The crowd responses may be distracting at first, but if you hang on I think you'll feel enlivened by the spontaneity and maybe feel you're *there* at the talk, not just reading another self-help book all alone.

Audiences laugh a lot in John's lectures. I cut most of the *"(Audience laughs.)"* from the transcripts, but I left them in when I thought it might be unclear that John had offered something as a joke and when the audience laughed with whole-bodied delight.

It is fitting that the audience be recognized as part of John's talks on recovery because, as he has taught many of us, recovery is something that happens, one day at a time, *with other people.*

Why Men Can't Feel
And The
Price Women Pay

Hello. I'm John Lee. Thank you for coming tonight.

As I was driving over, I thought how incredibly good it felt to be getting to do what I love — which is talk about pain. *(John laughs. Audience laughs.)*

Let me say a word first to the women here. Don't be put off by the title of this talk. I'm going to talk about why men can't feel and the price they pay and the price you pay, but the truth is women can have trouble feeling, too. Though I've specialized over the years in men's issues and masculine psychology, nearly everything I say in this talk applies to women as well.

Because the problem begins before we are sexual beings. It begins in childhood — in infancy, a great deal of the time. We are born into this world able to feel everything, every feeling known. That's what a baby is: a ball of feeling. A baby's whole body is a receptor of everything going on about him or her. You touch them or put a light on them or make a sound and they move toward you or toward the light or the sound, because they feel something and that feeling comforts them. They know it's right to feel.

And then, at a very early age, the baby or child starts shutting down its feelings. The baby discovers the world doesn't respond to its feelings. Doesn't come when it cries. Doesn't surround it with gentleness and comfort. The child discovers the world expects it to shut up. Punishes it for feeling and expressing its feelings. Abandons it — which is the worst punishment possible.

Now adults tell themselves that it doesn't matter what you do to children, short of physical abuse, because kids are so adaptable that nothing hurts them. This is plain wrong. The truth is anything that isn't kind and gentle and quiet and attentive hurts a child, because the child feels so much. Most of us know this, if we've lifted our consciousness off the floor at all. The wrongs we do babies in their first two years cause them suffering the rest of their lives. And certainly cost them hours and hours of therapy trying to heal themselves.

Most kids learn that what they are feeling isn't right — can't be right because the world pays no attention to it, even punishes them for it. And who's the world?

Mom and Dad. Sure.

During the first few years — or maybe later, maybe as late as six or seven — children become aware that something's wrong with them. Something is badly wrong because their parents don't like them as they are. And what does the child do?

Simple: The child changes. The child goes to work on itself and turns its energy, its basic being — which is right here in the chest, in what the Hindus call the heart chakra — against itself and stifles what it really feels. It suppresses what it is and becomes a false self for its parents. Because it must have its parents' approval.

This is something we have to be clear about. Children must have their parents' approval. From Day One. If an infant doesn't feel itself accepted and nourished by the world, if it isn't held and cuddled, it will die. We know this from experiments done on monkeys. If the infant is slightly older and doesn't feel itself accepted, it is likely to be autistic or schizophrenic. If the feeling of nonacceptance comes later, after the child is four or so and has developed a basic trust of the world, then the damage won't be so great. The child will just be neurotic, like us here. *(Audience laughs.)*

Now I mentioned what the Hindus call the heart chakra, the center of our being. My feeling is that the center expands down into the stomach area, what the Hindus call the navel chakra, because I know that when I feel things they go down into my belly. I've had the pills to prove it — I used to think about buying stock in Rolaids and Tums.

This space here *(John holds his chest and stomach)* is where we live. It is the area where we feel our selves. I'm not being mystical. I'm telling you what you can feel yourself.

This is the place we first felt our connection to the world — like an electrical connection. The line went out from us and plugged into Mom. It was the umbilical cord originally, plugged into Mom. It was plugged into Dad, too, because at first we couldn't separate them — they were our whole world. We had this electrical line, and it shot into us and powered us. We took our energy from Mom and Dad. And that's the way things were supposed to be.

Is this making sense so far?

Well, most of our mothers and fathers weren't whole enough and confident enough to keep empowering us through our childhoods. They didn't have the courage to let us be or become the selves we really were. They had grown up in families where they were forced to be the children their parents needed them to be, and they forced us to do the same. What they needed — and here's where the tables get turned — was our energy.

They needed us to spend our energy to become the children they needed us to be in order to feel good about themselves. They needed power from us. They needed us to fill *their* empty chakras — convince them they were a good mamma, a strong dad, whatever.

And here I want to change the metaphor from an electrical line delivering power to a drinking straw delivering nourishment. And I'm going to talk specifically about my experience and my mom.

She was like us: She came from a dysfunctional family. She was the child of an alcoholic, and because she was, she married my alcoholic father. Now my mom, because of her emotional problems, had a great big straw. And when I was young — hell, as long as I was around — she would take that straw and stick it in me and go "slupppp!" when she needed to.

Some of you are going, "What?"

I'm telling you what happens to every child in a dysfunctional family.

Mom needed energy from me and from her other kids, so she took it.

Moms and Dads do it all the time. She said, "Here's Mamma's little man! His face so shiny and his smile so big. I know I can always count on him. He'll take care of me."

I was probably five at the time. What was I supposed to say?

She hugged me and squeezed me and said, "Oh, I could just eat you up!"

Like the witch in *Hansel and Gretel.*

Do any of you know what I'm talking about? Raise your hands so the others can see.

O.K., a few. The rest of you are saying, "I ain't gonna raise my hand about nothing. Maybe I get eaten up."

So energy is sucked out of us to feed another person's image of herself or himself. More energy is taken from us, suppressing what we really are, our true selves. And what do we feel, those of us with straws sticking in us?

We feel like straw people — empty. Empty and tired. We're not sure of what we really feel.

From our neck down we shut down. We are dead at our core.

Now, I have to say this is particularly true for men. We're the ones, generally, who can't feel. Most women can. They were traumatized just as badly as we were. They were physically and sexually abused and psychologically ridiculed and rejected and suppressed, but still most of them can feel. Why is this? How come they're so lucky? That's what we'd all like to know.

Part of the reason, certainly, is cultural. Girls and women are allowed to be more emotional than boys and men. It's all right for them to express some of their real emotions. You go walking in a grocery store, down at Safeway, say, and if you see a woman taking Cheer and Pepsi off the shelf with tears running down her cheeks, you don't think much of it. Maybe you think, "She probably feels better for crying." But if you see a man crying in the same situation you think, "Uh-oh, danger. Better tell the store people so they call the guys with the nets."

We were taught so screwy as kids. We were taught *big boys don't cry.* You want to know why men can't feel? There's the reason in four words. We were taught whoever is toughest and holds in the most pain will get ahead.

I mean, you men here, did your dad ever come up to you and say, "Son, if you want to cry, have at it. I'm going to be here for you no matter what. You can cry your eyes out and you're still going to be my son and I'm going to love you and be here for you. There ain't any amount of tears can make me go away."

Hell, my *mom* didn't say anything like that, let alone my dad. She didn't say it because if I had cried like that it would have reminded her of her pain, and she would have had to feel her life. And if she did, she'd have been sobbing too, and we'd have both lost control. In my family you couldn't lose control. It wasn't safe. Somebody could have got killed.

As I say, most women still can feel. Part of the reason is different social conditioning. And part of the reason, I think, is physical. Myself, I believe in the body. I believe the body knows our true emotions. Men can shut down their heart chakras and go dead. But women can't. They have their periods, and they're always aware they can make babies. They have to pay some attention to what's at their center.

But what happens to men — and not only men, some women too — what happens when we feel the core of our being is empty? Huh? We knock and knock on our heart and nobody's home. What do we do?

Well, we move our attention elsewhere on our body. We move north or south. Or north *and* south, up and down. We move *both* directions, trying to compensate for our deficiency in feeling and our pain. Somewhere between the ages of zero and four I moved up north into my head. I had determined that the only way to survive the madness of my family and numb my pain and suppress the hole at my center was to get up into my head and control things.

All the men I work with, whether in group or consultation, say the same thing. "Yep, John, that's where I went, right up in my head, and I'm not coming down because it's not safe. *(Laughs.)* I'm not coming down and you can't make me. So just leave me alone and don't go talking about feelings and that stuff. My wife told me I had to come here, but that doesn't mean I've got to listen."

This is what men say. You ask them a really painful question and they answer from their head. For example, you ask them how they feel about their fathers. Ninety-nine times out of a hundred they'll clear their throat and say, "I've thought about this a good deal, John — the pluses and minuses. I've decided he tried as hard as he could. Basically, he meant well. He worked real hard to put bread on the table and send me to school. He had his problems — who doesn't? But I reckon he did the best he could. And that's how I feel about Dad."

You see why women have so much trouble communicating with men?

The woman says, "How do you feel about me?" The man says, "I think you're terrific."

The woman says, "Do you want to have a baby?" The man says, "Well, I don't know. I guess this is a good time."

The woman says, "Sweetheart, how about that sunset?" The man says, "I don't think I've ever seen a better sunset."

Men go up into their heads because it's safe there. If I hadn't gone up into my head, I might not have survived childhood. Because my family was plain crazy. That's the bottom-line truth.

Now if you had asked me five years ago whether my parents were crazy, I would have said, "No, I don't think so. I suppose they weren't much different from other parents. Anyhow, that's water under the bridge. Spilt milk — no use crying over it."

In other words, I would have been in denial about my parents and how I felt toward them. But now I can say, "Hey, those folks were crazy. And I hated and hated and hated them. It's not that they were *bad*; they were sick. Because they had been raised by alcoholics and didn't know diddley-squat about having a kid. They were 18 years old, for God's sake — give me a break."

How many of your parents were under 20 when they had you?

See, a good number.

(A man says something.)

She was 16? Yeah. I had aunts who had kids at 16. Can you imagine how much damage I would have done if I'd had a kid at 16 or 18? I mean, I would have done major damage at 30. At 37, I like to think now maybe a child could do more than just survive with me, because I've done so much work.

So, to survive, the men went up into their heads. They learned control. They learned to watch other people's behavior and figure out safe responses. If Dad was a little drunk, humor him along. Talk about sports. If he was *big* drunk, run away! If Mom was in one of her moods, nod your head and bat your eyes and sympathize.

Okay. Twenty years later, this boy is 27 years old, and a woman tells him she's looking for a sensitive man — someone who can feel his feelings. Well, this guy doesn't know his feelings from a shovel. All he can do is run away. Or nod his head and sympathize.

Now I said that men who were empty in their heart chakra moved their attention on their body north or south. Up to their head, or down to their genitals. That's a decent word, huh? — genitals. *(Audience laughs.)* In my family it was a given that we didn't have genitals.

The closest most men come to having a feeling is when they are screwing. You women know this — you listen to them while they're at it.

That's part of the reason men like it so much. It feels a lot like feeling.

But actually it's often just another way of numbing themselves down, suppressing the fact that they *aren't* feeling. Underneath, there can be a deep emptiness.

You see, those of us with a hole at our center — women
and men — have got to find a way to fill it up. When we
learned we were disconnected from our parents, it hurt so
much we fled to our heads or our genitals, but we still had
this emptiness in us. And it hurt so bad that we started looking for things to stuff in it and make us feel whole again.
We're still looking, most of us.

What have you used to stuff your hole?

Let me give you a short list of what I've used.

Women. That's my Number One. Because women are legal
and plentiful and can laugh at your jokes. I was never much
on cocaine because it wasn't plentiful. In Alabama I couldn't
figure out where to get any. But women — there are lots of
women in Alabama. I came to Texas and found there were
even more women. That was reason enough to come to a
bigger state, I think. I sort of had to come, because I already
had a reputation in Alabama of being an asshole.

So: Sex. Rock and roll. Work. Reading. TV. Drugs — mari-
juana. The '60s finally made it to Alabama in 1974, so marijua-
na was plentiful.

Beer. I would just take a funnel and plug it into the hole
here in my gut, and I'd pour in a six-pack at a time.

Any of you ever done that? Just numb your heart and gut
down with beer?

I love beer, still love beer, but I stay away from it.

(A woman asks a question.)

TV? Sure, I'd be about to have a feeling and I'd plug the TV
in right here in my belly and numb myself out. You knock
back four hours of television and you ain't going to feel a
thing. You know: *(Deep voice)* "Aw, honey, I'm tired. Can't we
just go to sleep? It's too late, honey, David Letterman's gone
off. O.K. O.K. Let's turn off the light and see what happens."
(John makes snoring sounds. Audience laughs.)

We stuff our emptiness because where a parent should be
in us, sustaining us, there is a hole. How many of you know
what I mean? Raise your hands if you know you have a hole.

Nearly everybody here. The ones who don't raise their
hands, maybe you had a functional parent.

I can't imagine that. I can't imagine anybody coming to a lecture of mine who had a functional parent. *(John and audience laugh.)* So I imagine you're probably still in denial or else you made up your mind before you came tonight that you weren't going to raise your hand to a damn thing.

But if by some chance you had a functional parent, I want you to see me after this talk because I'm going home with you!

Those of us who are empty, we don't feel anything much. We don't dare feel our emptiness because it'll hurt too much. We suppress it.

If you ask us what we feel, we'd probably say we feel a little depressed. Depression is an absence of feeling. Depression is *suppressed* feeling — feeling medicated away by alcohol or drugs or work or sex or some other addiction.

I was working with a client today who almost cried four separate times in the session. But he couldn't let the feeling out. He had to hold it in. Can you imagine what that does to your body's energy, stuffing that feeling down day after day? You wear yourself out keeping from feeling.

Now this man is educated. He has pain from his father's death and his mother's death. He has a great deal of love for his son and for his wife. He couldn't experience the pain he felt over his parents' deaths, and guess what he couldn't experience either? His love.

Feelings go together. If you repress one, you repress them all. If you use energy stifling sadness or anger, your joy will be stifled too.

Last week I was in Phoenix working with a client who had just got a call from a daughter he hadn't seen in eight years. She was a little girl when he divorced, and he lost her. She called him three days before Father's Day. I said, "How does that make you feel?" He said, "I don't feel anything. It's funny because I know I should be happy."

Well, he and I did some work and got him to feel. We had him replay the day before, and the tears started coming. And then the laughter, and both of them together. He hadn't been able to feel the joy of having his daughter call because for eight years he hadn't allowed himself to feel the pain of losing her.

Now, women, if I use my energy all day to hold down my anger, my pain, my joy and my fear, then when I get home that evening, what am I going to want to do?

I'm going to want to get some energy from you. I'm going to try to stick my straw in you and go "slupppp!" Give me some life.

Have you had this happen? You're feeling full of pep until somebody close comes up and hits you like a Mack truck with their problems, and after about 30 minutes you're exhausted. You don't have the energy to cook the bacon he's just brought home. Anybody had this experience besides me?

(Audience comments.)

Good, good. I like to know I'm not totally nuts.

You know what happened. You dropped your boundaries and let somebody get their hit of energy from you. And why did you do it? Because that's what you'd been trained to do. You did it because you found yourself in a familiar situation.

Familiar — the word comes from family.

You dropped your boundaries because that's what your family trained you to do as a child.

How many of you women gave energy to your dad?

Some of you.

How many to your mother?

Some more of you.

How many to your little sisters and brothers?

Well, that's pretty much all of you.

What we're talking about here are addictive relations. Most addictions — to alcohol or nicotine or food or drugs — are a one-way street. But *people* addictions can be two-way. Many of us go around with straws sticking out of us, saying, "I can take care of you." Many of us go around needing someone to suck on.

I can go into a room of 20 women, one of whom is looking for someone to take care of her, and I'll be drawn to her. We'll be sitting there talking and all of a sudden she'll whip out her straw and "slupppp!" And I'll think, "By God! I've found me a soulmate." Soulmate Number 307. *(Audience laughs.)*

I've had a bunch of them. That's one thing I like about the New Age people. They're big on soulmates. These New Age men come to me all the time and say, "I've met her, John, my soulmate."

And I say, "How long have you known her?"

"Three days."

"Three days, and you're talking about living together?"

"You bet. Because I've known her in other times and lives." *(Audience laughs.)*

Yeah, I want to say, "There's a reason why you feel you know her. You just met your mamma or your dad."

That's why my mamma married my dad. Because he was a drunk like her dad. If she hadn't found him, she'd have found someone just like both of them.

Okay. I've told you the bad news. Now, how do we empty people get our feelings back? How do we deal with this hole in us?

I'll tell you one thing absolutely guaranteed: We've got to stop numbing it down. We men have got to stop trying to fill it up with women. They don't want to be stuffed into our hole. They hate us for it. And the same for you women who stuff yourself with men.

We have to stop anesthetizing, medicating, doping ourselves with all the things we've talked about — plus some more like caffeine . . . Valium . . . nicotine . . . therapy. *(Audience laughs.)*

Yep, when I find I've been going to a therapist three times a week for 52 weeks, I know I'm running from my problems instead of facing them.

What does it mean to face your problems? It means to feel them. And when you do, there's going to be tears and anger and pain out the kazoo. Everything you've kept down is going to come up: memories, sadness, wounds. Now I'm not suggesting you welcome pain or encourage it — no reason to be a masochist. But you don't deny it or run from it. You're not afraid of it.

You come down from your head into your body and experience the pain. Let it lead you as far as its power holds.

The problem is, nobody wants to do this. We've spent our whole lives avoiding it, and then some weirdo like me comes along and says, "Go down into your body and feel the pain."

And you say, "Man, are you kidding? I was down in it when I was six, and it hurt like hell. Can't I do some fancy drug like Ecstasy that will make it all disappear and open my communication channels and fix me up in a month?"

No.

"Can't I follow a guru or do a spiritual trip that will take all the anger I have at my mom and dad and cleanse it in the Celestial Light?"

Nope.

You have to go down into it, and most people won't. Like the guy today who couldn't cry. I said to him, "Why won't you go down into your pain?"

"Because I'm afraid," he said.

"What are you afraid of?"

"I'm afraid I'll go crazy. I'm afraid I'll start crying and never stop. I'm afraid I'll lose control. I'm afraid my wife will leave me. I'm afraid it would disconnect me from my family."

I told him he was in a safe place. I told him feelings are nothing to be afraid of; they are just feelings, not acts. I would have liked to tell him that he is already disconnected from his family because he is disconnected from himself. That if he doesn't deal with his pain, the things he fears are more likely to happen. He *will* go crazy. He will lose control. His wife will leave him. His son will hate him.

He wasn't ready to feel his pain now. But he will be. Next time or next year. Whenever he gets over being afraid of losing control and being thought weak and unmanly.

Because, as I told him and I tell you now, you *can* get your feelings back. You can't be seven again — or 17. You can't have the innocence you started with. But you can feel everything that's in you.

You can get back your energy and your boundaries. Most important, you can get back your *self*. You can fill your chakra with your self.

You know this hole right here in your chest? As an infant, this was meant to be filled with God, Mom and Dad. But at age 37 this hole has to be filled with God and me. I'm not a kid anymore. Mom and Dad aren't supposed to fill it.

Don't you catch yourself wishing sometimes, deep down in your heart, that your mom and dad would come and be the mom and dad you never had? You know, when times are tough? And you say, "Goddamn, I wish I had a dad. I know I'm 50 and I know he's dead, but he ought to get up from that grave and come bail me out. I'm going to keep suffering and making only $9,000 a year so he'll know how much I need him to take care of me, as he never did."

Well, Mom and Dad ain't coming. They didn't back then. They won't now. My dad barely knows where Texas is. He can't climb out of his alcohol to come. Even if he could, he couldn't fill my hole. If he could fill it, he'd be willing to. So would my mom, even more. But they can't. They aren't supposed to. Neither are all the women in Alabama and Texas. This hole is mine. It's me.

I'm going to close with a story.

Once upon a time there was a man who thought he loved a woman very much. And he went to her and said, "I love you very much." And she said, "What do you mean by that?" And he said, "I love you very much and I need you." And she said, "What do you mean you need me? Why do you need me?" And he said, "I want you to marry me." And she said, "Why do you want to marry me?"

He couldn't answer any of her questions. Because what was talking wasn't his love for her but his emptiness. The woman understood this and she went away. They didn't live happily ever after.

The story isn't over. The man was sad but this time he didn't give himself over to drink and drugs. He didn't look for another woman to fill up his hole. Instead, he started to feel feelings he had hidden. His pain came up, and his sadness and grief. He understood that what he needed, what he had always needed, wasn't that woman or anybody else, but himself. And at the end of a lot of work, he had that self as never before.

And if, perchance, the man and the woman were to cross paths again and fall in love, and if the woman were to say,

"Why do you want to marry me," now the man had an answer. And the answer might be silence, but the woman would know it was the truth.

All right, that's enough. Let's take a ten-minute break. Then I look forward to your comments and questions.

Saying Goodbye
To
Mom And Dad

Thank you for coming tonight. I don't think I'd go out on such a foul night to hear anybody talk about *my* parents.

Now all of us know how much influence our parents had on our lives. Like me, you may wish it wasn't so. Like me, you may have spent a lot of time and energy denying it.

People I meet in my counseling and workshops come because they want to deal with here-and-now problems. They say, "I'm doing such and such" — drinking too much, fighting with loved ones, being depressed — "and I want to stop."

I say to them, "Okay. Which of these things did your parents do?"

And they say, "Look, I'm a grown-up. Why do we have to draw my parents into this? The less said about them, the better. I just want to get my life together."

The problem is, I don't know any way of getting our lives together without dealing with our parents.

In my workshops I ask people to write down what their problems are — what keeps them from being happy, what impedes their relationships with people. I have them list their problems as fast as they can, as many as they want to. Some people list five things and some people, like me, list 72 and run out of time and paper to write on.

Then I ask the people to go back and read over their problems and put down an M or an F beside the ones their mother or father also had. Now, very few people — and I suspect most of them are in denial — very few people come up with a list where every problem doesn't have an M or an F, or both, beside it. It's like somebody said: "Children don't take after strangers."

Kurt Vonnegut, who isn't one of my favorite writers, says that children are born spies. They are watching all the time to see how to *be*. How to be an adult. How to be a man. How to be a woman. How to love another person. How to get your way. How to be angry. How to make up.

And the object of our earliest and deepest spying was our parents. When we were infants, our mothers were all women to us, our fathers were all men. They were godly creatures performing miracle after miracle. Bringing food and music into the room. Opening the window so that a breeze came across us. Driving a car that made the buildings move and then stop. Mom and Dad had powers so vastly beyond our own that we thought whatever they did must be right and necessary.

If they didn't come when we cried, if they didn't hug us, if they didn't let us be with them, something must have been wrong with us. If they got drunk and shouted at us, it had to be our fault. If they hurt or abused or abandoned us, we must have deserved it.

Parents have got an awful advantage on their kids. And they all abuse it — they can't help but. I don't believe in Original Sin, but if I did, this would be it.

So now you see why it's so tough to say goodbye to Mom and Dad. They are the only gods we ever knew. They are the first and strongest loves of our life. It doesn't matter how much we hate them, loathe their values, despise the harm they did us and others, we still love them.

And if we hate our parents — and I hate mine, I hate their guts for what they did to my sister and brother and me — we hate them *just because* we loved them so much. We loved them so much we can't bear the disappointment they caused us.

And if we don't want to say goodbye, and most of us don't, it's because in a very real way we never *had* our parents. They weren't there for us as we needed them — accepting and encouraging us just the way we were. If someone tells us, "Say goodbye to your parents," we say, "Don't ask me to do that. I'm not ready to. My dad's been gone nearly all my life — I don't begin to understand the man — don't ask me to tell him goodbye."

We still hope that if we hold on long enough, Mom and Dad are going to behave like Mom and Dad should.

That's a pretty familiar strategy, huh? — waiting for someone else to get healed. *(John speaks in a piping voice.)* "If I just hold on and keep treating him right, I just know it's going to work out. He's got worlds of potential. Yes, I know I've spent 14 years of my life on him, but he's really made progress. I'm going to love him so much he'll have to get fixed. I'm smart, I'll figure it out. I'll take some more classes. I'll do the Dale Carnegie course!"

It's the same thing with our parents. Half of you, maybe more than half, are still waiting for your mom and dad to be the mom and dad of your dreams. You behave the way you should to give them the opportunity to behave the way they should and take care of the little child they didn't take very good care of back in the '40s and '50s.

You go home at Christmas, thinking, "This is it, Mom and Dad — one last chance! You booted the ball on Labor Day and Thanksgiving, but I just know you've — " *(Audience laughs.)*

You're home about five minutes and your mom's messing with you about your hair or car or boyfriend or your daughter's bad language. And you think, "She's not much different than what she was five Christmases — 25 Christmases! — ago. Now how is that? Man has walked on the moon, America lost a war to skinny people in black pajamas, the Catholics said it was okay to be cremated, and my mother still thinks all the rules of living were handed down on *Leave It To Beaver*." *(Audience laughs.)*

It's very simple: we don't want to say goodbye to Mom and Dad because we don't want to be cut off from them. Our connection to them has always been tenuous at best, and we're afraid that if we say goodbye it might just be severed and we'll go floating off into the ether. With nobody to love us.

Now that's the frightened child in us thinking. But we've all got a lot of that child in us. In my workshops I sometimes say to people, "You've got a Mom ghost inside of you and a Dad ghost inside of you. If I took Mom out and set her over there against the wall and took Dad out and set him at the back of the room, what would be left in you?"

And sometimes people say, "Nothing."

They feel they would be empty. They feel they are empty shells. I know, I've felt it.

You see why we've got to say goodbye to Mom and Dad? We've got to discover who we are. We're not just a compilation of Mom and Dad's best and worst traits. They tried to make us that. They didn't let us find our own selves and be proud of whatever we found. They tried to make us *them,* just as their parents tried to make them into them.

(Audience comments.)

Right. Or they tried to make us what they wished they'd been. They said, "Either we'll make you into one of us, or we'll make you into something we never could have been."

But they didn't let us just be who we were.

So we can't let go of them. Here's the sad truth: parents who can't let go of their children have children who can't let go of their parents.

And the more dysfunctional the family, the truer this is. I'm the child of an alcoholic parent. At about age two, I started studying my father. By age five I'd decided, yuck! I wasn't going to be anything like that man. When I was maybe seven or eight I can remember him smoking and drinking up a storm and shouting at me, "Boy, if I ever see you smoking and drinking like me, I'll tan your fanny the color of peanut butter. I never want you smoking and drinking."

And I thought, "Amen! I will never smoke or drink. I swear to God." Because I knew the pain my father caused. I'd *felt* it.

Okay. Then along about 15, 16 years old, what was I doing? Smoking like a chimney. And when things were bad at home, as they always were, what was my response, as soon as I could get outside? "Gimme a drink."

I was doing exactly what I hated more than anything else. Exactly what I swore to God I'd never do. And why?

Why? That's an honest question, friends.

(Pause. Nervous laughter from audience.)

Well, not really, because I've got an answer to it.

(Audience laughs.)

I was smoking and drinking because it connected me to my dad. I was partly doing it because it would make him mad — which would at least mean he was paying attention. But partly, too, because it was a way of being *like* him. He'd get mad and then he might say something like, "Well, at least you're my boy. A chip off the old block. *My* dad told me never to smoke or drink, too. Ha, ha, ha."

And I could laugh along with my dad, feeling that he accepted me. It felt good. Smoking and drinking, I could numb my pain and at the same time feel I belonged somewhere. I had the makings of a hell of an addict.

I've given you the main reason why we can't say goodbye to Mom and Dad. They didn't make us strong enough in ourselves; they kept us dependent.

A lot of us still feel threatened by our parents, even today. Even if we're 30 and 40 and 50 years old. Even if our parents are 20 years under the ground. If this was a workshop and we were crying and carrying on, about half of you would be eyeing that door to see if Mom and Dad were coming through it and might catch you.

Right? To see if Mom and Dad were going to catch you telling all the bad stuff they did to you. And you know what Dad would say: *(Gruff voice.)* "Get back to your room! You don't go around badmouthing your parents. We put food on the table and clothes on your back and sent you to college. You ungrateful whelp! Get out of that workshop! And wipe the snot off your face."

They can still get you, huh? The little child inside of us is always looking over its shoulder to see if Mom and Dad approve. Now at a lecture like this, that's not a big problem because you can say, "Mom and Dad, cool it. I'm not doing anything but sitting here listening to this jackass beat his gums. I mean, the TV's broken at home and I've seen all the movies in town — I don't have anything else to do. I'm not crying or beating a pillow or yelling and cussing. It's sort of like church, only they take the collection at the door."

You see, what we're doing when we worry about Mom and Dad coming through the door is what we've always done. We're trying to protect them. To keep them from being hurt. In dysfunctional families, the kids are all the time called upon to parent their parents. I had to protect my mother from my father because he was an alcoholic and a rage-aholic, and I had to protect both of my parents, especially Dad, from our friends and neighbors because I didn't want them to know what was really going on.

Now the reason we parented our parents wasn't only to protect them. We meant to set them a good example. It was obvious they didn't know how to parent *us,* and we thought maybe we could teach them, we being age five or six at the time. "Now I'll show you, Mom — watch. I say *(Piping voice)* 'How you feeling, honey? Would you like me to bring you something?' That's what *you're* supposed to say, Mom. And then I answer, 'Why, that sure is nice of you.' "

But mainly we were protecting them. How many of your moms had a tough life? Raise your hands.

Okay. How many of your dads?

Nearly everybody in the room raised their hand once. Many of you raised them twice.

Sure, a kid thinks, "They've got it tough. I don't want to make it any harder on them. I'll be what they want. I'll forget about my feelings."

I found myself trying to protect my mother the other day. You know I wrote a book, *The Flying Boy,* about my dysfunctional childhood. Well, that came out a year ago, and just recently I've been making a series of tapes of my lectures. So a couple of weeks ago my mom called and said, "I'd like an order of your tapes. The whole set."

(Audience laughs.)

I said, "Mom, are you sure?"

She said yes.

I said, "Mom, I've got to tell you, I'm a little nervous about this. I say some things that are fairly harsh, you know, I wouldn't want you to take them wrong."

She said, "Well, son, after reading that book of yours . . . *(Audience laughs.)* I don't know that anything would shock me."

I said, "Well, you know, Mom, I've done some work since the book and I've come up with more stuff."

I was scared because my mom's in recovery, been in it for about 16 months, and I didn't want to hurt her work. I told her that outright. I said, "I know I'm being co-dependent here, but I kind of want to protect you. There are things on the tapes that are hard for anyone to listen to. But I'll send them because you say it's time you heard them."

So I sent the tapes. And the last few days I went around thinking, "Phew-eee! She's got the tapes by now and she still hasn't called. I don't have a mom anymore. I'm a 37-year-old orphan. Boy, is she pissed at me."

Today I told myself to stop imagining trouble and call her up. And I did — I called her. It was a beautiful conversation.

She said, "I listened to the tapes, and they opened many doors for me." She said, "When you spoke about how we have a hole in us and people come and suck energy out of us, I know I did that to you and your brother and sister." She said, "I didn't know what I was doing at the time. The years when your father would come around, at the end of the day, I just felt depleted. You've given me an explanation now that I can work with and live with. I'm real thankful. I enjoyed those tapes a lot."

I just listened. I was thinking, "God, this is a woman who's been healed." It was strange. I thought, "She's stronger than me." *(Laughs.)* You know, "She's getting ahead of me!" *(Audience laughs.)*

We keep thinking of recovery as a race, and that's wrong. We're each running for ourselves.

I was scared for my mom to hear the tapes. I wanted to protect her from what would hurt her, the way I'd always done.

We don't want to say goodbye to Mom and Dad because we don't want to hurt them.

But there are still other reasons we don't say good-bye. One is, people keep telling us to forget about our parents and what they did. These are well-meaning people — very Al-Anonish types, for those of you who go to 12-step meetings. You start talking to them and they say, "Just let it go. The past is past. Just turn the page over." That's a favorite phrase: "Turn it over."

They say, "Resentment will only drag you down and hamper your recovery." And if you're really feeling it and start crying, they say, "There, there," and they give you a pat and a box of Kleenex. *(Audience laughs.)*

Which means: "Keep it dry, buddy boy."

Now I'm not in favor of resentment, but what I'm saying in all these lectures is that each of us has got to *feel . . . again . . . exactly* what it was like growing up in our family. And be angry. Be sad. Be hurt. Be abandoned. Feel all the feelings that come up, and then, *after* we've felt them and owned them, let them go. Turn the page over.

But until we do that, until we've felt everything on the page, we're not ready to turn it.

And those nice folks at the meeting who say "there, there," to shut you up, they will tell you *they* have let go, but it ain't necessarily so. Some of them are threatened by what you feel. They haven't felt their pain fully, and they're afraid of its power. Many of them are still full of rage. You say something like, "What I'm feeling today is totally pissed at my mom and dad," and they say, "Shut up! Don't say that in this meeting! You're full of resentment. Work a step on it."

And you think, "Gee, if that guy's in recovery, I'm not so bad off."

People try to do to you just what your parents did: make you nice and accommodating. *Prematurely nice.* That guy who told you to shut up was prematurely nice. I was prematurely nice for 34 years.

My friends now say, "John's angry. He's really into anger."

And I say, "Yeah, I'm into anger because I've got a whole lot of things I'm pissed about."

But for 34 years I was Mr. Nice Guy. You ever met me? "Hi, I'm Mr. Nice Guy, and I'm prematurely nice. How you doing? Oh, I'm fine, fine, I'm always fine. How you doing? Can I help in any way at all? I love being walked on. I don't know how to say no."

Mr. Nice Guy goes home at the end of the day and beats his dog and curses his wife or vice-versa, right? Or you remember the E.A. Robinson poem about a Mr. Nice Guy named Richard Cory? He was rich and handsome and sweet to everybody, and he went home one summer night and put a bullet through his head?

I want to tell you that it's fine to be pissed off, hurt, sad, resentful, whatever you feel. These are all just feelings, and everybody has the right to feel what they feel and to express their feelings. No more Mr. Nice Guy if that's not what you feel.

If you feel pissed off at your parents, feel that. You're not harming anybody, and nobody should blame you for what you feel. You can feel safe because you *are* safe.

Now as a child, you weren't safe. If I had gone to my father when I was six or seven and said, "Dad, I've got a feeling I want to share with you. Dad, I'm pissed off at your alcoholism." *(Audience laughs.)* Well, I would have been sent into lunar orbit.

But that little child in us who couldn't acknowledge its feelings then has to feel them now. I don't know any way around it. Because if we don't feel them, we can't let them go. We'll stay locked in our old patterns, which is a point I'll get to in a moment.

First, I want to make sure you understand that when I talk about the importance of feeling what your mom and dad did to you, the mom and dad I'm talking about are dead. They're ghosts. They live in the painful patterns they taught you and you bring into the present, but they're gone.

Now some of you will disagree. "That's not true for me," you say. "My dad is still acting like a horse's ass. My mom is still on my case."

If they are — and I don't doubt it — that's because you're still playing the child role with them. And you're seeing them with your child's eyes, *angry* eyes, *sad* eyes. That's all right if you want to do it, but your real quarrel isn't with that 65- or

75-year-old man and woman you call your dad and mom today but with your ghost parents of 1950 and 1960.

You don't have to work with your parents in the present if you don't want to. The best thing you can do may be to stay away from them for a while, so as not to confuse them with their ghosts.

And if your parents *are* dead, that doesn't matter. Their ghosts aren't dead, and your quarrel is with their ghosts.

Our parents' ghosts are alive and well in us. I hear my ghosts talking to me all the time. *(Gruff voice)* "Get up, boy, you're late! You're wasting daylight." I jump up out of bed, and start going. Then I think, "Hey, wait a sec. It's *Sunday.* I don't have to work, Dad. I can sleep some more." And Dad replies, in me, "You're always sleeping, boy."

How many of you think of yourself as lazy?

More than half the audience.

How many of you remember your mother or father calling you lazy? *(Audience laughs.)*

See there? More than half the audience.

You know how I know you're not lazy? Because lazy people don't come to lectures on miserable Wednesday nights trying to learn how to heal old wounds. And yet a lot of you think you're lazy. Because your mom and dad planted that idea in your little brain — in a little center called the lazy center. And when you sleep late, that little center goes "Beep, beep, beep! Someone's still asleep!" And then the voice comes on, *(Gruff voice)* "Get out of bed, you lazy slob!"

You know, I even *sound* like my dad.

We have all these ghosts inside us waiting to jump on us and tear us down. How many of your folks used to say, "You're not very smart"?

Hmm, that's not as big as lazy.

How many of you were called *stupid?*

(Audience laughs.)

Your folks liked the direct method!

What happens to you now, of course, is when things are going tough you say things like, "Boy, if I wasn't so dumb, I could figure this out."

That's your parents talking to you. They've put a dumb center in your brain and you activate it . . . to tell you how dumb you are.

People aren't dumb. We know everything we feel we really need to know. Sometimes we can't make up our minds about something, but that's because we were kept from respecting our own feelings.

Until we let go of the patterns of thinking our parents planted in us, we're doomed to repeat them. We'll keep leaping out of bed when it's Sunday. Keep postponing that vacation we feel we don't deserve and can't afford. Keep throwing money away on junk we'll never use — an exercise set and an electronic organ — to make the neighbors gawk. Keep drinking and chasing new lovers.

We have to do it. If we don't get rid of the patterns, we have to try over and over again to complete them. You know why?

Well, it's like when you're in a car listening to a catchy song on the radio and you arrive where you're going and turn the song off before it's finished. What happens? You have to whistle the song or hum it or say the words, or you won't get it out of your head for the rest of the day. You have to complete it.

Everything in us seeks a closing, a completion. What we haven't finished with our parents we have to try to finish with the other people in our life. We play out our old patterns with our spouses or our bosses or strangers on the street.

But it doesn't work because they're not our ghost parents. They look at us and think, "What the *hell* are you doing?" *(Audience laughs.)*

And we look at them and think exactly the same thing — because they're not doing what *they're* supposed to. They aren't our parents and don't know the pattern.

Or maybe they do! Maybe we chose them because they *did* know it. That's what children of dysfunctional families do when they pick somebody to marry; they choose someone with similar psychic, emotional and physical needs. And the marriage is a sharing of dependencies. The woman says, "Yes, I mother my husband. I'm his mother — I know that. But he's my daddy, too." And man and woman change roles back and forth, each getting a shot at the role they feel they have to play.

Haven't you done that in your relationships?

It comes from not saying goodbye to your ghost parents but instead trying to relate to those parents through the people in your life today.

And if you've got children, the people in your life today include them. Instead of letting them be who they are, you can turn your children into ghost parents, a little mom and dad — or a little you — trying to complete the pattern in your head.

That's not a nice thing to do, is it, boys and girls? Not at all. That's what was done to us. That's why we're sitting in this room.

If it hadn't been done to us, I wonder what we'd be doing tonight?

If the weather was better, I suspect I'd be playing putt-putt golf. I've always thought I'd like that game.

Until you say goodbye to your mom-and-dad ghost parents, you're going to be playing out the patterns they taught you.

Now I've just said that if you haven't said goodbye to Mom and Dad you're probably in a co-dependent relationship with your husband or wife or lover. This doesn't mean you ought to say goodbye to your husband or wife or lover — just your parents. You can recover from your dependency on your ghost parents and stay with your partner *if* your partner is willing to work on their dependency. Your partner needs to be as equally committed as you, equally willing to look at their own problems.

It's likely your partner won't be. We co-dependents were programmed to pick somebody we could count on not to get well. They'll talk about doing it. They'll promise to do it as we're headed out the door. And maybe they will do it for about six months, since we didn't leave. But then as soon as we've dropped our boundaries and our bags, they'll stop working. Because they've got us again. And they know exactly how far they can go before we pack our bags. When we do, they'll make more promises, and the cycle will go on.

Any of you been in a cycle like this with a spouse or lover? Yeah, nearly everybody.

You've got to hope your partner will see that they need to do the work for themselves, because they're living in pain, not for you and not because you're walking out the door.

If you're in a relationship, turn to your partner and say, "I'm going to work on my problems, and I hope you'll work, too. Not with me; with yourself and on yourself. I'm going to heal myself. Nothing is going to come between me and my recovery — not even you, sugar. That's how committed I am."

And if your partner won't do the work and won't quit the patterns he or she is playing with you, well, that's their problem. You can live with it. But the question is, do you want to? Because living with those patterns means you're still living with Mom and Dad at age 37.

You want to live with Mom and Dad till you die? I wanted to get out at 17. I don't want to be still with them at 47, 57, 67.

But I encourage you, if you're in a relationship, stay there for the time being, because whatever work you don't do in this relationship you will have to do in your next one. Recovery isn't all or nothing, now or never, though we tend to think so. See it as a process. Give your relationship time to change and then make your decision.

And if you're not in a relationship, decide tonight that you're not going to go out and find your parents all over again — that you're going to wait and work on yourself till you're somebody, in yourself, that you're happy to spend the rest of your life with.

Now I know working on yourself, in or out of a relationship, is harder than finding a new lover who will ease your pain for a little while — till the old patterns show up. But working on yourself is the only thing that will free you from the patterns and make *sustained* happiness possible.

Our parents didn't teach us to expect happiness that would last. They believed, and they made us believe, that life was a struggle where we could expect to lose many more times than we won. Where we'd have to work our asses off and still not be satisfied. "Life is hard," they told us. "You can't trust anybody — except to wreck your life."

I don't think life is hard. Not unless we make it so. And I don't think people will wreck our lives unless we let them.

The secret to happiness, friends, is to carry our own pain and not carry other people's. Since childhood we've been carrying our parents' pain. And when someone like our father or mother comes along, we've said, "Hey! I know you. We're soulmates! Come on, hop up, I can carry you. I got my parents and their pain, but I can . . . Whoa! You're a little bit heavy there, but I gotcha. Hang on. Whew!"

Right? Women carry men's pain. Men carry women's. Children carry their parents'. Parents carry their children's — I imagine that's the hardest to get free of.

And it's heavy! Other people's pain is heavy. I can carry my own pain pretty easily — my pain's heavy, but it's not that heavy. But to carry my mom's and dad's and the woman I'm dating . . . .

Well, I flat don't do it any more. Not when I'm in my right mind.

And you don't either. Everybody in here has started letting go of other people's pain and paying attention to their own. You came through the rain tonight because you're ready to say goodbye to Mom and Dad. I've told you that the way to do this is to feel your feelings about your parents and your childhood. Every time you do that — every time you let a feeling come up and be felt, a memory come up and wash through you — you're saying goodbye. Every time you don't — every time you stifle a feeling or a memory — you're trying to clutch on to Mom and Dad.

By coming tonight, you show that you've got a *good* Mom and Dad in you. That good Mom and Dad said to your inner child, "Come on, honey, we're going to a talk tonight. Come on, it'll be good for us. You'll be fine."

You could have chosen to get drunk or overdosed on TV, but you chose to be a good parent to yourself. And this means that your mom and dad, bad though they were in some ways, were good, too.

When you say goodbye to the bad ghost parents in you, you'll keep the good parents. You'll make them stronger. And with study, with observing other people, with working on yourself, you'll become even a better parent for your inner child and make that child stronger.

You can make that child bloom in you as soon as you stop treating it like dog scum, the way your ghost parents treated you. Until you say goodbye to those parents, that child in you is going to say, "I ain't coming out. It's no safer now in 1988 than it was in 1958. I'm not coming out till you get rid of those mean, critical, hypocritical tyrants."

And if your inner child doesn't come out, you're not going to be nearly as creative as you can be. Not nearly as happy and confident. Not nearly as much in love.

But those inner children aren't going to come out if we keep working till we can't stand, or overdosing on TV, or drinking alcohol and coffee and smoking up a storm, or hanging around people who aren't good for us.

If they don't come out, we can't realize our potential. We need our child selves working in tandem with our adult selves. As adults, our duty is to get a job that's healthy for us. Make rational decisions about living right and taking care of ourselves and our family, if we choose to have one.

The child in us is in charge of our *free* energy, our intuition, spontaneity, lightness, ecstasy, joy.

You see why we haven't seen much of those good things lately? Because we've been abusing the child in us.

I really believe our inner child is our highest self. Our *real* self. He or she is the person we were before society, in the form of our parents, put our masks on us.

That child was connected to God — still is! And our adult self isn't. At least our adult self doesn't *feel* like it is. That's the problem with the adult self: It doesn't feel much.

Our adult self says, "God's hard. God's far away. Man's alone. Life's sad. We've lost the connection to God."

To which the child self says, "You're ridiculous. What do you mean *connection* to God? I *am* God, you fool! *(Audience laughs.)* I am spiritual life. I am part of every rock I play with, every cloud I look at, everything I taste and hear and smell. I am God."

The child self wants us to play. Next Wednesday night, maybe putt-putt golf, huh? *(Audience laughs. Applause.)*

Well, we're out of time. What I'm saying is, let go of your ghost parents and take care of your child self. And you're doing it, we're doing it — we've been doing it. We can just do it better.

Okay, we'll take a break and come back so you can have your say.

Co-dependency —
How To Fight It
(A Talk In Six Parts)

1. Recognizing Co-dependency

Welcome, I'm flattered to have so many of you here. I'm a little nervous, too. I suspect about half of you are writing books on co-dependency and you've come to check out what the competition is saying. *(Audience laughs.)*

I'm not kidding. Books are being published on co-dependency almost before they're written. Co-dependency is a real hot topic these days — like AIDS, the other social disease of the 1980s.

You hadn't known they were similar, had you?

The difference between co-dependency and AIDS is that AIDS is a new disease and co-dependency has always been with us. In a way, we don't need new books on co-dependency because nearly all the great books are about it.

Look at *Oedipus.* Talk about repeating your parent's patterns! *(Audience laughs.)* Or *Medea.* Her husband, Jason, is running around with other women, and Medea's ashamed, her self-esteem is zero, she moans and moans that she can't live without him. Jason promises to reform and doesn't. So Medea chops up their children and cooks them in a pie, which she serves to him. That is a seriously dysfunctional family.

The greatest writer on co-dependency I know is Ralph Waldo Emerson, who died 100 years before the disease was named. "Whoso would be a person must be a nonconformist," he wrote — which says it all.

Actually he wrote, "Whoso would be a *man* must be a nonconformist," but I didn't want any of you women to be put off. *(Audience laughs.)*

You see, I'm co-dependent on your approval.

Now Emerson wasn't popular when I was in college because the critics said he lacks a "tragic sense" — as he does. But I'm hoping to get rid of *my* tragic sense, so I like Emerson just fine.

One thing that interests me about Emerson is that he's called the most *American* of our philosophers — because, you know, he preached self-reliance. This suggests to me that we Americans have always recognized somewhere deep in us a problem with co-dependency and the need to fight to be ourselves.

Isn't that true? In our society we gain prestige by what other people think of us. Most of us don't get ahead because of who our families were or how much money they had in the bank or where we went to college 20 years ago. We get ahead because of the opinion other people have of us now. Today. As we interact with them. That's what Dale Carnegie said, and Benjamin Franklin before him.

And the problem for us is that trying to win other people's approval, win friends and influence people, as the man said — we're going to lose who we are.

In fact, we lose it all the time.

That's the first thing I want to say about co-dependency: Everybody is co-dependent some of the time. With some people. In some circumstances.

You can go live in a cave in New Mexico with no one but a dog and you'll probably start trying to guess how the dog feels about you.

And all of us who believe there's some meaning in the universe, we're co-dependent on God, whatever we call God. We realize we don't have full control over our destiny.

So everyone is co-dependent sometimes. But I better say what co-dependency is. There are lots of definitions running around. Here's mine: Co-dependency is a disease suffered by a co-dependent person. *(A few people laugh.)*

I thought you'd like it.

And what's a co-dependent person? A co-dependent person is someone who depends on someone else or something else to make him or her feel better.

Repeat: A co-dependent is a person who depends on someone else or something else to make him or her feel better.

Now I could have used a more roundabout definition. Like: A co-dependent is a lifeguard who drowns trying to save everybody in the bay. Or: A co-dependent is someone who says, "I'm O.K. — if you're O.K."

Question: How many co-dependents does it take to change a lightbulb?

Answer: The co-dependents can't do it because they've grown accustomed to the dark.

A co-dependent is the woman who came up to congratulate me after my brilliant two-day workshop on co-dependency in Santa Fe. She said, "John, this has been great. It's changed my life. But I've got to ask you something. My boss at work is driving me crazy, and now I'm finally going to tell him so. What do you think he'll say?" *(Audience laughs.)*

I said, "I'm sorry, lady, I'm in the wrong business. I'm going to the Outer Hebrides and raise sheep."

She said, "You don't understand. I just want to know before I tell him."

I bet she did.

A co-dependent says, "If you take my job away, I'll die." My father used to say that all the time.

"If anything happened to your mother, I'd die. There'd be no reason to live." He used to say that, too.

That's real love, huh?

People think it is. How many of you have broken up with somebody who treated you like dirt and then, when you get away, they come after you and say, "I gotta have you, baby. Look, I ain't kidding. I mean, I'm about to *die!* I know I

treated you bad, but I can change. I'll go into therapy. I'll learn
what dysfunctional means. I'll even learn to spell it. I got lots
of potential."

Does he love you?

Did my father love my mother?

Well, it's hard to say. He said he'd die without her, but he
said he'd die without his job, too, and he hated his job.

He was co-dependent on them both. Or to use another
word, he was *addicted* to them, just the way he was addicted
to alcohol.

What's your addiction?

Mine is work. I've given up the alcohol, given up cigarettes,
given up pot. Haven't quite given up women yet. I don't know
if I really want to kick that habit. But I sure would like to kick
the work habit. And I mean to do it. The IRS says I owe them
some money, so I tell myself I'm working to keep them happy.

The truth is, I'm co-dependent on my work. I feel good
when I feel other people are counting on me.

Addiction, pure and simple.

Co-dependency is addiction — an addiction like any other.
And our understanding of co-dependency starts with research
that's been done on the disease of alcohol addiction.

Here is a little co-dependency history — or maybe folklore,
I don't know which. One of the famous clinics in Minnesota
was sending home alcoholics who had been dried out like
bones on a beach. As part of their recovery these men and
women had lived in halfway houses where they could have
gotten booze if they wanted to, and they hadn't done it. But
when they got home, nearly all of them went back to drink.

So the operation was a big success, except the patient died.

You can hear the people in the clinic joking, "Yeah, they'd
be fine if we didn't have to send them home. They catch the
disease there. Ha, ha."

And then somebody realized: "Hey, wait — that's it! It's not
only drink they're addicted to. There's something in the home
environment. Something that reinforces their dependency.
Something in the way the family members interact with one
another. If we are going to help the alcoholic, we have to help

the other members of the family, too, or change the way the alcoholic relates to them."

And that's how therapy for co-dependency — for dysfunctional family dynamics — was born.

Which brings us to tonight.

You're here because you want to believe there's some way to embrace your life, fill the emptiness you feel at your center, stop making such a mess of your relationships.

There is a way. It's hard. It takes work and watchfulness and suffering and patience. And it won't make you 100 percent well for ever and ever, any more than alcoholics are ever "cured" of their disease.

But it will change your life. It has already changed your life in bringing you this far into recovery.

2. Recognizing Denial

Alcoholics start recovering when they admit they are alcoholics.

The same is true for co-dependents.

And just as alcoholics have great trouble admitting their addiction, so do we. This is because we have been taught from childhood to be liars. To lie to our parents. To lie to ourselves. To hide who we are from everyone, including ourselves. To deny reality. To deny what we feel.

You came home from school and Dad was there, muttering in the backyard. You asked your mom whether he was drunk, and your mom said, "No, he's not drunk. He's just feeling poorly." Her eyes were red and moist, but she said she hadn't been crying. "Now go to your room, hon. I'll call you for supper. That's a good boy. Everything's going to be fine."

And you went to your room and stared out the window. *Going* to be fine? But she said everything *was* fine.

Or you were in your room and heard shouting downstairs. You came down and said, "What's wrong?" And your mom and dad stood there, steaming. Your dad said, "Nothing's wrong. Everything's okay. Get back to your room."

And you were so young then you thought, "I must be *weird.* I felt something was wrong because Mom and Dad were shouting at each other, and nothing was."

Your mom and dad thought they were protecting you by lying. But they weren't. They were teaching you not to trust your feelings. They were teaching you that big people get by in the world by saying things they don't mean, hoping to make other people feel better and think better of them.

Denial of reality. My father denying his alcoholism. My mother denying her addiction to the sedative drugs that numbed her to where she could tolerate her pain. Both of them denying their fear and guilt and misery in the marriage.

And what was I denying? Everything! Just as I was going to do for the next 25 years. I was hiding in my room, with my record player turned up, hoping Jesus would come soon. "Please, Lord Jesus," I was praying, "let this be The Time!"

I was six or seven, and there didn't seem to be any other way to straighten out my life. I knew things would get worse as I grew up — look at my parents! — and I would start sinning like them, and still be terrified and unhappy.

Children learn to deny who they are and what they feel, because the people in authority over them deny these things. Let me give you an example.

When I was little my family and I would go on trips, and I'd get real nervous, as co-dependents do when we'd go to a new place. Co-dependents have to be in control, and we know we're going to lose it for a while in a new place. No sooner would we start driving than I'd have to pee. I'd tell my dad, and he'd say, "You don't have to pee. You *can't* have to pee — you just peed."

Now it was true I had just peed. My dad wouldn't start out without making sure all the children were drained. So when I was little, I thought he must be right; I couldn't have to pee again. "I really thought I needed to, but I guess I don't."

When I had an accident or two and started talking back and saying I did too need to pee, I got a swat on the head.

Or I'd tell my dad I was hungry.

(Gruff voice.) "Shut up! You ain't hungry. I'll tell you when you're hungry."

Or I'd cut myself and be bleeding. "Oww, that hurts, Ma!"

"That doesn't hurt. That little cut? That doesn't hurt my big boy."

We're trained to ignore what we really feel.

(Gruff voice) "How are you feeling, John?"

"Fine, boss. I feel fine."

"Then I can count on you for some more hours?"

"Ahh, I'm doing 55 hours this week already, boss."

"Now, John, are you telling me you're tired? A great big guy like you?"

"Well, no, boss."

That's the way we live, we co-dependents. We even lie when it would be just as easy to tell the truth.

Why? Two reasons. One, we were brought up to take care of other people. Two, we never learned we could tell the truth and not suffer for it.

Now it's hard to stop denying what's true if you've built your life on denial. The temptation is just to *deny* . . . you're denying. *(Audience laughs.)*

Yeah, it's tricky. Even starting to deal with denial is tricky if you think about it. Because how can you recognize you're in denial if you're in it? You can't, right?

"You're in denial."

"I am not!"

"See! You are, you are!"

(Audience laughs.)

That's the kind of conversation people have — kindergarten level. Because, emotionally, we're age three, most of us.

Just imagine what a sane place the world would be if somebody said "You're in denial," and the other person answered "Yes, I certainly am." *(Audience laughs.)*

Well, it doesn't happen. But you can't begin working on your problems until you come out of denial. Many people go through therapy for years and years with their denial system intact, the therapist unable to crack it.

I tell clients all the time, "Gee, I'd really like for you to go to that Adult Children of Alcoholics meeting or Co-dependents Anonymous to supplement the counseling we're doing." I don't tell them they *have* to go. I try not to be authoritative, because we neurotics have had enough authoritative people in our lives.

If the clients are people-pleasers, as most of them are, they'll say, "Yeah, okay, I want to do well in therapy. I want you to appreciate how hard I'm trying, Dad — uh, Doc — uh, John. I'll go."

Next session, they'll come back and say something like, "Well, I went there because I knew you wanted me to and I'm a goddamn people-pleaser. But I'm going to put my foot down. I'm not going to another 12-Step meeting. It didn't work for me, and that's that."

I ask them why it didn't work.

"Why?" they say. And they whip out a list of reasons they've written down. "I jotted down a couple of hundred reasons. Like, you know when you say, 'Hello, my name's Bob,' everybody turns and smiles at you and says 'Hi, Bob'? Well, that makes me puke, just to start with. *(Audience laughs.)* It's so mushy and phony. And the Lord's Prayer at the end? Some of the people there could be atheists or Buddhists, right? They'd be offended. And how about the feminists? You know, 'Our *Father* who art in heaven . . .' ? I just can't sit still for sexism."

Co-dependents find endless reasons for staying in denial. There's one reason they come up with that I sympathize with, and I'm going to tell it to you so you can use it. They say, "I don't want to go to those meetings, ACoA or Al-Anon or CODA, because whatever you say you are, you become. So if I say I'm a co-dependent, I become one."

And I say, "Well, damn it, man, you *are* co-dependent. You're one already, or you wouldn't be seeing me."

"Yeah, but I don't want to absorb additional negative spiritual vibrations." *(Audience laughs.)*

The New Age — don't you love it?

In fact, those spiritual vibrations from other people are what is going to help you and me and all us co-dependents, alcoholics, children of alcoholics, druggies, sex addicts, gamblers and weight-watchers toward recovery. We were wounded among other people, so we have to heal among other people.

Now co-dependents who are far enough out of denial to know they need help usually accept one-on-one therapy. They may not love it, but they certainly prefer it to group therapy.

Why? Because they know that being around other people who are co-dependent will mirror back their problems, and this terrifies them.

They're right. Group therapy is going to bring up stuff much faster than private therapy will. Go to a 12-Step meeting, and you're going to have to face every demon in your closet.

So you better figure out reasons to stay away. Come to safe lectures like this instead. Or read books. I hang around the self-help section in the bookstore, and I'm all the time running into you folks.

I say, "How are you? Don't I remember you from the lecture?"

"Yeah," you say. "After your talk, I went out and bought 32 books."

"That's nice," I say. "That will give you stuff to read. Why don't you come to a workshop?"

"Naw. Those things don't work for me. I'm a Buddhist."

Self-help lectures and books and private therapy can all be ways of prolonging denial, but at least they are attempts to come to grips with one's pain. Most people don't make the attempt. They just keep running away.

They come to therapy for a while. They work, they agonize, and then they vanish. I bump into them on the street two weeks after they skipped their last appointment.

"How you doing, Ralph?"

"John, I'm doing great! I got me the best new girl in the world."

"But you just broke up with —"

"I know! Isn't it great? Life just keeps giving me all these wonderful women. I swear I think it must be God working on my side, bringing me these women."

"Ralph, that's not God. That's you. You're drawing them like flies."

"Really? You think so?"

I tell him I think so. I don't say that he's drawing them like flies because he's like a big wad of horseflop on the ground.

(Audience laughs.) He's stinking and they're stinking, and everybody's senses are so damaged they like the smell. They begin dating and just like *that* they're soulmates.

That's the thing with us co-dependents: We don't have relationships — we take hostages. We say, "Umm, boy, she looks good. I have *got* to have me that! Where has she been all my life?"

I'll tell you something about co-dependents in case you ever date one of us. You go out with us two times, and you're *ours.* If we like you.

And we don't even have to like you very much! Because we're not picky. If you smile pretty good and look pretty good . . . you know, not too many tattoos . . . and no criminal record to speak of — just a *small* record, not the FBI list — we'll take you. Because we can't be alone.

Two dates will do it.

Now people say, "John, you're exaggerating. We went on four dates before she asked me to move in." *(Audience laughs.)*

And what happens when the bloom of romance wears off and the old patterns show up?

Mostly, we change partners. The patterns stay the same — I'll talk about patterns later — but we change the faces. The bed hardly gets cold.

Co-dependent as we are, we always think a new partner is going to fix us up once and for all. We'll be healthy! We just need a later model.

"Hello, Woolco? What have you got in women these days? Yeah, on sale — I don't want to pay full price. $29.95, eh? Now, is she going to remind me of my mom or dad? *(Audience laughs.)* That's okay. I've had enough moms for a while. But you always got moms in stock, right? There's a lot of us count on it."

3. Two Ways To Know If You're In Denial

I want to tell you two ways you can know if you're in denial about your co-dependency. The first is, if you find yourself saying things you don't mean. This applies whether you're in your bedroom or your business office; if you find yourself lying, you're in co-dependency. You're taking care of someone else's feelings.

This is what most of us do most of the day: We spend our energy (1) repressing our feelings and (2) trying to guess and cater to other people's.

I look out at you in the audience now and I see your reactions and I think, "Oh, God, she thinks I'm an asshole. She thinks, 'This is the dumbest talk I ever heard.' And *he's* practically asleep! I gotta wake him up. Now careful — no cursing, John. Don't use the F word. Nobody's going to think better of you if you have to say 'fuck.' " *(Audience laughs.)*

Sorry about that.

Now that's the way we co-dependents think — all the time second-guessing other people, taking care of them.

You know what the Existentialist philosopher Jean-Paul Sartre said about folks who live this way?

He said we're living in hell.

He did. He said, "Hell is other people."

I agree. Trying to live your life as you think other people want you to is like being one of those zombies in the movies that isn't alive and isn't dead.

Hey, that's it! A new support group for co-dependents: Undead Anonymous!

The second way to know if you're co-dependent is to pay attention to your body. If your shoulders are tense, if your lower back is sore, if your stomach's twisted in knots, if your head aches and your butt is numb, if you can't breathe more than a cupful, you're in co-dependency.

Now this is something generally overlooked in co-dependency treatment, but it's of major importance. The body is a barometer to the spirit.

I can tell when I'm in co-dependency now because I finally have my body back. I had to work my tail off to get it back, and I can still lose it pretty quick. I'll feel a slight pain in my chest, and I'll know, "Uh-oh, something's wrong." And I'll try to change what I'm doing.

I treat myself just like I was an alcoholic or drug addict.

Sometimes I'm on the wagon. Sometimes I'm drunker than hell with co-dependency.

And when I am, the way I recover is through my body. I do exercises, jog, pump weights, dance around, swim, sing, scream, do deep breathing, get a massage.

I get out of my head.

Yep, to get your body back, that's what you have to do. And the problem with lectures and reading and most kinds of therapy is they're all head-centered. That's why I try to be funny in these talks, because when people laugh it puts them back a little bit in their bodies. Crying does the same thing, of course, but who wants to cry? *(Audience laughs.)*

Actually, I'm just being flip there. I love crying. I'm so glad the feminists came along and said the men could cry and the women run conglomerates. The problem with crying in a talk like this — well, there are two problems. First, you can't control it. Laughter stops right away, but crying goes on and on. Second, laughter joins you to other people, and it feels like crying separates you if there's no one else crying.

Now I've talked about how hard it is for most people — especially men, but some women too — to stay in touch with their bodies. This is particularly true for people from dysfunctional families. We can detach from our bodies quick as a wink. I've seen several of you all do it since I started my talk. You're just gone out the window and soaring down the street. Saying, "I'm not listening to this B.S. My wife said we had to come, but she never said I had to listen."

One reason we lose track of our body so easily is that it was abused when we were children. It was beaten. Molested. Ridiculed. Raped. Pinched. And I don't know what — tortured!

And the least of these can cause a trauma. Cause us to check out. Cause what the psychologists call "dissociation" from our bodies.

You know what it feels like right here in your stomach when some person you respect and believe you should be safe with tells you you're ugly. You're short. You're ears are funny. Your nose is gross. You're too brown. Your penis is teensy-weensy. You're hairy. You've got no tits.

It wipes you out.

I've heard parents tell their kids: "You're worse than plain." "I'm ashamed to have a child that looks like you." "It's an embarrassment to see you up on stage." "You ought to lose some of that weight." "You ought to do something about your pimples."

Parents shaming their children. Telling them, "You're not good enough the way you are. I want you to be different."

How many of you heard that as a kid?

Yeah. About half of you. The others can't admit it because it's too painful.

Our parents abused our bodies. And not only Mom and Dad. Older sisters and brothers. Grandpa and grandma. Uncles and aunts.

I had an uncle who was one of the most abusive people in my life. I hung around with him all the time, though, because he was a little bit less abusive than my dad. He would let me ride on the tractor and ride the horse and go to ballgames with him. My dad wouldn't do any of that with me. My uncle would, but in the process — and I didn't know this till I was nine years old, and then I suddenly realized it and I'm glad I did — in the process he would all the time make fun of me. Laugh at my ears or my lips or my warts or my handshake or something. I didn't care, because compared to what my dad did, which was beat me, it was mild.

Co-dependents spend a lot of time playing the comparison game. They come up to me and say, "Well, yeah, John, I can understand if someone beats the hell out of you, you detach from your body. But nobody beat me. They just made fun of me."

I'm telling you that your father, who told you you had an ugly body, abused you just as much as my father did, who beat my body. You have your pain and I have mine. And who can say my pain is bigger than yours? There's no way to measure pain — thank God! — because it's personal. And no one can be sure that you weren't hurt worse than I was.

The abuse we received made us co-dependent. And not just co-dependent toward the people we loved who abused us. It started our co-dependency toward the world. Because we were abused, we meet the world expecting the worst. We say to ourselves, "What are other people going to think and feel about me if my own kin didn't accept me, didn't love me as I was? What can I hope from folks I don't even know? I've got to be careful. I've got to watch them like a hawk and see if I can't scope out what they think of me and how they mean to treat me. And maybe I can get on their good side."

That's it, huh? Pretty sad.

We've got to take our bodies back from other people. We've got to pick up the pieces and "re-member" them. Embrace them. We've got to build a pride we never had before.

A couple of weeks ago my mom gave me a picture of me when I was six. I'd forgotten it, but now it's my image of what I hope to be. *(Laughs.)* I'm wearing high shoes of the kind right-thinking parents bought their kids in those days — Buster Browns, they were called. I'm wearing a tee-shirt and jeans. And it's interesting: I wear the same exact clothes these days — right down to my lace-up boots.

But what's most remarkable in the picture is my smile. It's a really *happy* smile — self-satisfied, even a little smug. That child hadn't been mortally wounded. That child never can be destroyed.

I keep the picture in my office now, and when a friend comes in I say, "See that picture? That was me when I was six. I was the cutest little rascal."

We've got to build a pride we never had before.

4. Patterns And Breaking Patterns

I said I was going to talk about patterns, but I'm not going to. I've got your $10 and I'm going home. Good night!

(John starts exiting. Audience laughs.)

See, that's what I'm preaching — breaking patterns. Spontaneity!

You don't like it, eh?

(Audience laughs, comments.)

There's nothing vicious about it folks. It keeps the juices flowing.

Patterns are death. Or rather, patterns are a way of being neither dead nor alive. Undead Anonymous is full of people living out their patterns.

When you were a child in your dysfunctional family, you had to follow the pattern set out for you or very likely you wouldn't have survived. You had to play the false self your parents wanted because you had to have their attention and love. You knew you couldn't take care of yourself. That possibility never even crossed your mind. You *knew* you couldn't be abandoned. You had to hang in there regardless of the cost.

So you played along. You hid who you were — hid it so well some of us can't find it anymore — and pretended to be your parents' darling or demon, whichever they wanted you to be. Occasionally you'd try to sneak out a little of your real self but that was usually squashed right away.

How many of you knew by the time you were ten that your mamma and dad didn't like you the way you were?

Nearly half the room.

How many of you knew it by the time you were six?

Quite a few.

How many of you got the message, directly or indirectly, that you weren't even wanted in the first place?

About a third.

My mom told me a wonderful story. This was back before she got into therapy and recovery. She told me, "Son, I've always taken pride that you were planned for. You were really wanted."

And I said, "Wow. Is that right? Hey, I was wanted! Tell me more about that, Mom."

And she said, "Well, your dad and I were talking. He was about to be called up to join the Korean War. And we decided that if he went away and got killed, we would want a piece of him left behind." *(Audience laughs.)*

And I said, "Mom, do me a favor and hush up. This isn't going to help our relationship at all!"

She thought I was wanted.

That happened a lot. Babies born because the father might be killed. Babies born because the father wasn't killed. "Hey, let's celebrate! We haven't seen each other in three years. Let's have a kid!" *(Audience laughs.)*

Well, a lot of people were born for dumber reasons than that. Like "I forgot the condoms, honey."

(Piping voice.) "That's okay, honey, because I forgot the Pill."

I knew by the time I was seven exactly which self, which mask, would please my mother and keep me out of trouble with my dad. I knew what to say, how to move, how to complain, how to butter up and cajole.

I could tell what I looked like to them.

I could tell what they were thinking.

And the basic pattern of my life was set. My motive was to try to look better in my parents' eyes so that they'd like me more. So that instead of abandoning me they'd want to have me around. So that instead of withdrawing into drink and despondency, they'd be *there* for me.

What I learned to do as a child is what I've done as an adult. I cozy up to people — it might be you, it might be your pretty sister, it might be the postman — thinking, "What do I need to say? What do I need to do? How do I need to *be,* so that you'll like me? Should I stand on my head? Write a check? Be the best lover ever? Nod and shuffle and smile? What do I have to do to make sure you don't leave me? Just tell me and I'll do it. Only you don't have to tell me. I've got lots of experience — just let me guess.

"I've got a trunkful of masks here. Which one you want? The Sensitive Man? You bet I've got a Sensitive Man mask. Where is that sucker? Ah. Shooeee! *(Gestures to his face.)* Sensitive Man. You want some tears? Poetry? Social protest?

"You don't like sensitive men? Well, of course, that's fine. I understand perfectly. I agree 1,000 percent. Now let's see, you probably want the Strong Silent Type. Which I have right here, somewhere. Yup. Shooop! *(Gestures to his face.)* Clint Eastwood. Old Iron Balls. 'I'd smile but somebody's foot is in my testicles. And it smarts.' "

You women do the same thing. Playing the Earth Mother — you know, peasant blouse, no bra, good honest sweat. Or the High Fashion Lady with a pound of mascara and three-inch heels.

I could never figure out why you cared for us enough to do that to your legs. I guess it's caught you a few. I know my Sensitive Man caught me some.

We take on those roles, basically, because we don't want to be abandoned.

Which is the fear we've got to face, deal with and get over. The one who told me it could be done was Charles Whitfield in his book *Healing The Child Within*. He didn't exactly say it, but what I took him to mean was that an adult can't be abandoned. A child can be, but not an adult.

You may say, "Oh yes, they can. I was abandoned by my husband of 30 years." Or, "I get abandoned all the time."

No, you aren't abandoned. The *child* in you is, the needy child who craves caring for. But the adult you, who is capable of taking care of that child and all your other selves, isn't abandoned and doesn't feel abandoned. The adult you is always there, waiting for you to feel its power.

As an adult, the only way you can be abandoned is if you abandon yourself. If you don't let your fingers do the walking to call for support and counsel. If you don't climb into your car and drive to a friend or sponsor or therapist. Children can't do these things, but adults can if they choose to.

If you're getting abandoned all the time, my suspicion is that you're like I was: you *try* to be abandoned. If you're like me, you're addicted to abandonment. You wouldn't know what to do with someone if they *didn't* abandon you.

I'm not kidding. If someone we loved said to us, "I love you just the way you are. You don't have to change at all. You don't have to wear any mask. You don't have to worry in the least; I'm going to be with you for the rest of my life," we would say, "God Almighty, what have I done to deserve this, and how do I get out of here?" *(Audience laughs.)*

Right?

Sure, we'd be scared out of our shoes. "I'm never going to get rid of this creature!" I mean, what do you do with someone who just *stays* with you? "Hey, look, honey, can't you go away a little bit so I can chase you? I know how to do that. I mean, that's the pattern."

The sickness we're suffering from — whatever we want to call it: co-dependency, addiction, dysfunctional relationships, undead living — is a bit paradoxical. So long as people keep leaving us we know what to do; we follow the old script and try to win them back. ("I'll change, honey — honest.") That's what we did with our parents. We tried to win them back, away from work, booze, the TV, despair.

Of course at the same time that we try to win our lovers back, we complain — that's part of the script. We complain about how fickle and selfish and uncommitted they are.

"Why?" we sob on our friends' shoulders, "Why can't I fall in love with someone who can love me?"

Well, we've made sure to pick someone who *can't.* Someone like our dad or mom, whichever parent it was who was absent for us. Someone we can count on to run off, so we'll know how to behave.

A woman told me a surprising thing the other day. She said, "I just like to get in a relationship and have fun for 11 weeks — and get the hell out! You know, before all the mess starts. Because I know he's going to leave me, so I want to leave him first."

Eleven weeks — that's the voice of experience. *(Audience laughs.)*

Some people say three months. The romantics say two years.

Not only do we know that in the long run the relationship won't work, *we count on it.* We've decided that's the way life is for us. "I know what my patterns are," my clients tell me all the time.

"Okay," I say, "tell me what's going to happen in your relationship now."

"Well," the client says, "I'll do this and this and this."

"Yeah, and then what will she do?"

"She'll do this, this and this."

"And then what will you do?"

"I'll do this, and I'll say that if she does that again I'm going to eat her lunch."

"What will she say?"

"She'll say this and this, and have the locks changed."

"And what will you do?"

"I'll take back the credit cards."

And I tell the client, "You got it! You got it all laid out. You're not going to give that up for therapy. You wouldn't give it up for a million dollars. You know exactly what's going to happen. You two could just call a truce and not even go through it — just jump to the end of the script and save time."

It's a paradox. For children of dysfunctional families, so long as a relationship isn't working, it's working *perfectly*. The pattern is repeating itself. That's exactly what adult children want, because they are in control.

I say to my clients, "Okay, you know your patterns. What would happen if you broke them?"

"What?" the client says. "Break my patterns?"

"Yeah, what would happen?"

"I don't know."

"Well, think about it some. What would happen?"

They think about it some, and generally the bottom line is they don't know. They don't know so much that, rather than give up control of what they *do* know, they prefer to stick to the pattern.

It's not hard to know what our patterns are, but it's hard as heck to break them. Breaking a pattern is going to throw your body and mind into such a state of derangement that you may feel like a junkie giving up his drug. In a sense, you are; you're going cold turkey into the unknown. A ton of fear is going to come up, definitely. A ton of guilt, very probably.

Say you've been calling your mom and dad every week — on Sundays, when the rates are cheap — and you know how much your calls mean to them. Then you discover you have a lot of hate and anger toward your parents, and you don't want to talk to them. So you don't call. Then along about four o'clock Sunday afternoon, less than an hour till the rates go up, you begin thinking, "They're going to think something's wrong. Those old folks are going to worry. Dad's going to be pissed off because I made Ma get one of her headaches."

Guilt. It's a great force keeping us in our patterns.

I broke a pattern once, and I'm going to tell you about it because it still scares the shit out of me.

This woman I loved — I call her Lucy in my book *I Don't Want to be Alone* — and I were having one of our arguments. It was two o'clock in the morning. I got out of bed, put on my pants, walked out on the front porch, sat down and looked at the sky. I was steaming mad. I was deep in pain.

After a while I found myself thinking, "My God, how many times have I been here, on a porch in the middle of the night, my stomach in knots, with some woman raging at me back on the bed? I couldn't count them on all my fingers and toes. What's going to happen next, according to the pattern? I'll go back in and get my shirt and put it on, waiting for her to say something — which she won't do. Then I'll get my keys and go for a drive. I'll get back early in the morning. She'll still be in bed, and I'll crawl in and we'll go to sleep. When we wake up, mid-morning, she'll say, 'How're you doing?' And I'll say, 'Fine. I'm fine.' And she'll say, 'Want to talk about it?' And I'll say, 'No, it's over now. Forget it.' And we'll just keep going like nothing happened, only I'll be dead inside for a few weeks."

I looked at the sky and thought, "Arrgh! Why not something different?" And then I began sweating like a pig. Because I realized if I did something different, I wouldn't know what she'd do. My mouth was dry. "Don't know what *she'll* do," I thought. "Christ, I don't even know what *I'll* do!"

Then I thought, "Quick — do something different, or you'll do the same thing."

I jumped up and marched back into the bedroom and got into bed. I took a couple of deep breaths and said, "Hold me, please."

And you know what? Lucy did. I had my face down in her neck, her arms around me. I could smell her skin. She patted me on the shoulder. I thought, "This is good. Man, this is good! But shit, what will I do *now?*" *(Audience laughs.)*

We lay there a good while. I was reminded of something that happened to me as a child. I was maybe eight years old, riding my two-wheeled bike, and a big dog ran at me and I fell off. Well, I was across town and didn't know anybody, and a woman took me in and fed me cookies and milk.

And there in my bed 25 years later, I started crying. And I thought, "Oh, my God, I'm crying with Lucy. I've got this adult-child pain, and what's she going to think? What am I going to do next — wet my pants? I came in from that porch like gangbusters and next thing I'm dropping tears down her nightie. I can't be doing this."

But you know, with all those tears and uncertainty, I felt wonderful. I was alive. I had broken free. I had given up powerlessness and emptiness for a real shot at living.

5. Strategies For Pattern-Breaking

Let me give you three strategies for breaking a pattern when you're in a fight with a loved one.

The first is what I just did: Give up hostility, return anger with love, turn the other cheek. Of course, if the other person keeps punching you in the jaw, stop playing Christ and try another tactic.

Like the second, which is this. You say something like "Becky Sue" or "Bobby Joe" — that's what we say in Alabama, you know, because everybody has two names — "Becky Sue, I love you very much. I'm not abandoning you. I'm not leaving you. But I am going off now to work on what's going on between us. This is work I have to do by myself. I'll be back, I promise."

Now that sounds easy and reasonable, doesn't it? But to be able to say it you have to be fairly sure Becky Sue isn't going to have a coronary and die right there on the floor. You have to be sure that when you come back from having done your work, if Becky Sue has changed the locks and gone, *you* won't have a coronary and die on the floor. In other words, you have to know that both Becky Sue and you are adult enough to care for yourselves.

You need to have done the basic work on your adult-child abandonment issues. Because when you say "I'm going off now to do work on myself," the abandonment issue has got to come up, for both of you. Because you've begun a real relationship, where you don't have a fixed idea of how things are going to turn out.

Dysfunctional relationships perpetuate control and predict-
ability. Healthy relationships allow some chaos — though it's
usually safe chaos — and spontaneity.

So you go off to work on your problem someplace else —
that's step three. You've already drawn your boundaries by
moving out of the co-dependent confrontation. You've set
limits; you're not going to shout at Becky Sue or have her
slap your face.

Now you spend time with your Higher Power, your God or
Goddess, the Ground of your being — whatever you call it.
You exercise to get your body back, till you feel your strength
in every part of it. You call on the support system you've built
up: a friend who is in recovery, your 12-Step sponsor, your
therapist. You go to 12-Step meetings. You talk out your problem with people not involved in the quarrel and see it from a
perspective free of egotistical emotion. You come to realize
the adult-child issues this episode restimulated, and thus
you're able to break the pattern fully, because you see that
what happened now between you and Becky Sue is a repeti-
tion of what happened to you a generation ago.

Then you're able to go back and talk to Becky Sue and see
her as she is, not as a version of your mom or dad. You say,
"Becky Sue, let me tell you why I was so mad when you
arrived late. It had nothing to do with you. It's because I was
abandoned when I was six. My parents said they'd pick me up
at the movie theater and didn't do it. I stood looking at the
street for an eternity. There were all these big people around
— it was a Western — and I thought something awful bad
had happened to my parents. I was terrified. I was in shock."

Most likely Becky Sue can hear what you're saying. Ninety-
five percent of people could. She will probably take it without
offense, and your relationship can flourish. I calculate that
nearly every fight I've been in had more to do with me and
my history, or the woman I'm with and her history, than it did
with us in present tense.

Now it may be that while you were away Becky Sue worked
on her problem and found the reason she got so furious when
you yelled at her for being late. Your playing out your pattern
started a pattern for her. Behind your yelling she heard her

father yelling, "Do you know what time it is, girl? I told you to be home at 11 o'clock. You see the time now? After one! And you didn't call us. You know your responsibility — if you're late, you call!"

You and Becky Sue had your fight because you each were seeing yourself as a child and the other as a hostile parent. When you shouted at each other, you were simply repeating your old co-dependent patterns.

No. Break the pattern.

"I'll come back later when I've worked my problem out." It'll work unless the person you're dealing with is too dysfunctional.

What else about patterns? I want to say a couple of things fast before I forget.

When you give up living in a pattern, you also give up trying to control other people. They don't like you — too bad! They don't approve of your behavior — tough patootie! They offer you the last piece of chocolate, which you're sure they want — you take the chocolate.

See the person there in front of you, listen to the person, share with the person what's going on. Never mind what you think the person needs to see and hear — be who you are. Say what you want. Take the risk.

That's what intimacy is: saying what you feel and think when you feel and think it and not suppressing it because you're afraid of what the other person will think or feel.

Don't second-guess the other person and the other person's problems. Co-dependents are people-pleasers. We're always trying to fix people, heal them. Well, the other person's not broken — and if they are, we can't fix them.

If you want to know what they want, don't guess — ask them. Our culture has the weird notion that if you have to ask for something, it's no good.

(Piping voice.) "I want you to tell me you love me."

(Gruff voice.) "I love you."

(Piping voice.) "That doesn't count." *(Audience laughs.)*

(Piping voice.) "I want you to know what makes me *really* excited."

(Gruff voice.) "Great!"
(Piping voice.) "But I don't want to have to tell you."
(Gruff voice.) "How am I supposed to know, then?"
(Piping voice.) "That's *your* problem." *(Audience laughs.)*

Yep. As kids we spent half of our waking time at home trying to figure out what our parents needed. We got pretty damn good at it. I could see what my dad and mom needed at about 50 yards. While running! See it in the way their bodies sloped, the tightness across the shoulders, the frowns and smoky looks. "That means she just had a fight with Dad. I've got to do something to make her feel better." I'd try to fix Mom, fix Dad, fix my brother, fix my sister.

You see the omission?

I never thought about fixing me. Instead I turned to my addictions — from Jesus to Jim Beam.

It never crossed my mind that I could take care of myself first, because I had been taught this was selfish.

That's why we're here tonight — because it was ingrained in us that looking out for ourselves first was selfishness.

How many of you got that belief in your childhood?

Everybody in the room. Nearly everybody.

I think the truth is just the opposite. Your responsibility is you. If you have a hope of fixing anybody in this world, it's good old Number One.

And for those among us who are Christians, I don't think Jesus would disagree. He said contradictory things on this matter, if we accept all the sayings attributed to him. But the Golden Rule, for example, tells us to love our neighbors *as* ourselves. Presumably, then, we love ourselves first. Certainly we aren't told to love our neighbors *more* than ourselves.

We co-dependents have to turn the Golden Rule around and learn to love *ourselves* the way we love others. That will be plenty, and plenty hard for us.

"Honey, you're wonderful. I'm scum."

"You deserve love. I need to hurt."

"You should have a healthy relationship. Me, I should help you get one. Because you're somebody, and I'm negligible."

If we did to ourselves as we do to others — treated us with the same attention . . .

I mean, I've treated some people pretty shitty in my life, I admit it. But I can't think of anybody I've ever treated as shitty as I've treated myself. Not one person. I haven't hurt anybody near as bad as I've hurt myself. I haven't made anybody else's life hell on earth.

In a shipwreck, it's women and children first. In a decent society — which, incidentally, is a long ways from what we have in this country — those who can't help themselves are cared for. But in matters of the soul and psyche, I have to believe it's every man for himself, every woman for herself, and God will take care of us all.

6. Getting Better

How do we recover from co-dependency?

Well, we don't get well all at once, and we don't get well all the way. But we can get better. I've started getting better — I'm not well, but I'm better — and I bet you've started getting better, too. You wouldn't have been able to hear me out with such patience and attention if what I said didn't reverberate in your own experience.

What I want to say in closing is real simple — like everything else I say. Even simpler.

It is that you're more likely to get better faster if you attack your illness from several directions at once.

Co-dependency should be dealt with on the spiritual level, the physical level, the emotional level and the psychological level all at the same time. If you don't do this, if you approach it on just one or two levels, you will make progress, but slowly, because your commitment won't have the intensity it needs.

For example, if you meet with your psychotherapist at 11 and then eat three hamburgers and 50 French fries for lunch, you probably won't make much progress that day. Or, say you do a 12-Step program but neglect physical exercise — you won't be moving ahead as quickly as you could.

You have to be active and healthy in your spiritual, intellectual, emotional, interpersonal and physical life. It all has to go together.

You need proper diet, nutrition and exercise for the physical self. You need prayer, meditation and affirmation for the spiritual self. You need counsel, support and intimacy for the emotional self. You need stimulation and variety for the intellectual self. And, for all these selves, you need relaxation and reflection.

Say you wake up sad in the morning. I often do — it appears to be a characteristic of people with depressive tendencies. So what do you do? What a child does when he or she is sad. You cry. You have the biggest cry you can.

And *then* you eat a damn good breakfast. And you walk to work if you can. And it's a nice long walk, if you're lucky. You meditate or say affirmations to yourself as you walk or ride the bus. When you get to work, you climb the three flights of stairs instead of taking the elevator. You call up a friend you count on to say how you're feeling and find out how they're feeling. That afternoon you buy yourself a book you've been wanting to read and then go for a swim at the Y.

That's what you do, because you're serious about recovery.

What most people do when they wake up sad is to swallow their feelings and sit on them. Then grab a cup of coffee and a doughnut. Then bump their car along among a thousand other cars. By mid-morning they're deep in depression. By mid-afternoon they're exhausted, waiting for a drink to pick them up for a moment and let them further down.

No wonder, then, when these people talk to God at the end of the day, their prayers — as e.e. cummings said — sound like *nevers.* "I never thought the day would end. *(Audience laughs.)* I never want another day like that. I'll never like my job. I can never understand my spouse. I never have any fun. My kids'll never grow up. I'll never get out of debt. I never asked to be born."

You, on the other hand, having felt your feelings in the morning and let them out, having eaten well, shared your deepest feelings with your friends and exercised your body and mind, are going to feel different when you take ten minutes in the evening to reflect on the day and speak with God. You'll probably say thank you. Say the day was good enough. Say you'd welcome a lifetime of such days. Say meaningful things happened because you worked to make the day rich and agreeable for yourself. Say each member of your family and all your friends and your colleagues at work are doing as well as they can to realize what is true and good for them. Say you are ready for whatever tomorrow brings. And will learn from it. And grow better. And say thanks again.

Now *I* want to say thanks again — to you, my friends, for putting up with this lecture series on co-dependency. I hope it's been useful. I want to thank you for your words and faces and love and support. I forgot to say this directly last Wednesday night, and I went home wishing that I had. I know it's a co-dependent thing to want take back last Wednesday and say thank you, but I'd like to do it.

Anyhow, *twice* as much thanks *this* Wednesday. God bless, and be careful on the roads.

What To Do
With Your Anger
And Grief

I want to thank you all for being here. You're brave souls, coming to a talk that says it's going to be on anger and grief.

I was thinking about this today, and I decided maybe the title shouldn't have said "anger and grief" flat out, because people would be scared.

These emotions scare people.

The emotions that *boast* of scaring people — fear, terror, disgust — have something exciting about them. They intrigue us. They offer a challenge. *Can you take this?* That's why people ride the roller coaster and go to horror movies. They want to be frightened.

Well, people don't want to be angry or sad.

That's what I should have titled this talk — "The Emotions Nobody Wants."

I've talked on grief many times and talked on anger many times, but I'm so slow I didn't realize the talks were saying the same thing until a few weeks ago. Tonight I'm going to give the talks together and see what happens.

Okay. We know the reason we avoid grief and anger is that these feelings involve pain.

Grief is a *felt acknowledgment of loss.* If you think about
it, life is nothing but a great big *losing,* childhood to the grave.
Losing the comfort of the womb. Losing the connectedness to
our parents. Losing Santa Claus. Losing the best dog a boy
ever had. Losing our first love. Losing the heroes of our youth.
Losing the hope we'd do something remarkable with our
lives. Losing our hair, losing our figure, losing our teeth.
Losing the children we brought into the world, who now
stand looking us in the eye.

When we grieve, we admit our limitations. We admit that
the march of time is tragic because it goes in just one direc-
tion. President Kennedy and Groucho Marx aren't going to
walk this earth again. And someday we won't.

If you really think about that, it doesn't make you feel too
brisk.

So we try not to think about it. We push loss away. We don't
grieve.

In fact, we *suppress* our feelings of loss. With the conse-
quence that all our feelings, positive and negative, become
depressed and we drag ourselves through the day, tired and
empty.

As for anger, we hate it even more because most of us were
its victims as children. We know from experience that when
somebody gets angry, somebody else is going to get hurt.
Beaten. Cursed. Ridiculed. Shamed. Maybe half of us here are
still in shock from the anger we experienced as children.
Don't ask us for a good word on anger.

Well, I'm going to say a good word for anger and for grief
right now.

Anger and grief are just feelings like other, happier feelings.
They don't harm anyone when they are felt and expressed
appropriately. They do harm only when they *aren't* felt, when
they are buried or medicated or turned into something else or
expressed improperly.

If we use them right, they can do good things for us.

Anger can get us unstuck. Rage won't — but clean anger
can. It can separate us, finally, from our parents. It can help us
disconnect from relationships that have gone dead. It can
empower us to burn the bridges of our co-dependency.

Grief, too, can help us get unstuck. When we acknowledge a loss at the deepest level of feeling, we let go of it for a moment. When we've felt that loss enough, we can move on. The loss will still be there. We will have to experience it again. But we won't be its prisoner.

Those of you who have read my *Flying Boy* know the thing that freed me from my dysfunctional childhood at age 34 and started my recovery was grief. Every day and every night for nine months — with the exception of eight days, according to my journal — I cried and cried and cried. The pain kept coming up, the memories kept coming up, the scenes of abandonment and suffering kept coming up, and I let them. I welcomed them. I felt them as much as I could.

I said to myself, "I don't know where this will take me, but I trust it because it's true. This is what my life truly was. Before, I was lying. Now I know the worst."

And I cried and cried.

Before I did this grief work, I was depressed maybe 85 percent of the time. Since, I've been depressed exactly one day. And that was only in the morning.

So you can't tell me grief is unhealthy. Grief gave me a life infinitely better than I'd had. On my worst day now I'm happier than I was on my best day then. Anger helped, but it was mainly grief.

In my consultations and workshops I see lots of people trying to feel their pain, both anger and grief. I see their feelings struggle up onto their faces and then swallowed back down. I see people make contact with a feeling, get ready to accept it, maybe even express it for a split second and then run away. They *fly* away from feeling. That's what I did. That's where I got the title for my book.

I ask these people, "What are you afraid of? If you let yourself really feel your anger or your sadness, what do you think would happen?"

And the answer is always the same. If I've heard it once, I've heard it 300 times.

"John, I don't know. I think if I let myself really go into my anger, I'd tear this house down. I might kill somebody. No one could live with me. I might go crazy."

Or:

"John, if I felt my sadness, I'd drown in tears. I'd never stop crying. My family would leave me. I'd go crazy."

Those answers are wrong. They're backwards. If people *don't* go into their feelings, their lives will keep on being drowned in tears and murderous fury. The folks they love will be *more* likely to leave them. They themselves will be more likely to get sick, physically and mentally.

You see, the problem is we don't understand the difference between healthy and unhealthy anger, healthy and unhealthy grief.

Unhealthy anger is anger suppressed, anger denied, anger unfelt.

Unhealthy anger can turn to rage.

And to hate. That's what hate is, according to my friend Dan Jones — anger unexpressed.

I said everybody fears anger, but it isn't anger we fear, it's rage. And with reason. Rage is the ugliest and meanest human emotion. Rage is the father throwing his infant child against the wall and killing her. Rage is the mother scalding her child with boiling water to teach a lesson. Rage is the husband choking the family dog because it snuck into the house. Rage is the driver who tailgates you for ten miles blowing his horn because you cut him off by mistake. Rage is the good church-goer who takes a shotgun and kills five strangers on the street, then blows his head off.

Rage is awful and has no decent place in normal human relationships. Not at home. Not at work. Not in public.

(Shouts.) "Goddamnit! Who left the fucking tricycle in the driveway? Shit!"

That's rage.

(Shouts.) "Who left the goddamn pantyhose in the sink?"

So is that.

Now people who get that upset about a tricycle or panty-hose are really acting out an old anger that they weren't able to express.

Those of us who grew up in dysfunctional families have been stockpiling anger since childhood. We tried getting angry at Dad when we were four, and we got whipped so hard we learned better. We talked back to Mom at five and were sent to bed without supper for that outburst. We saw we couldn't express our anger safely, so we learned to stuff it in a closet.

Maybe the closet was here, in our neck, so you can hear how full it is from our high-pitched voice. Or maybe the closet was down in our guts, which have so much pain in them they hurt us all the time. Or maybe it was in our sore back or our headachey head.

Wherever we put our closet, it got stuffed full of raw, unexpressed anger. And from time to time some silly thing — the dog coming in with mud on its paws, pantyhose in the sink, a car cutting in front of us on the freeway, our child being ten minutes late — is going to make the closet door blow off like the lid on a pressure cooker, and the angers of a lifetime are going to pour forth in rage.

When unhealthy, suppressed anger breaks loose, it is rage.

When unhealthy, suppressed grief breaks loose, it is self-pity.

(Sings.) "Aw, my baby left me, and I'm gonna stay drunk and lose my job and not shave and smell bad."

"I ain't worth shit. I'm the lowest, meanest, most despicable fart ever drew breath."

"She's a goddess. I'm cowflop."

Rage and self-pity are the classic emotions of the drunk. Some drunks, like my dad, mix them together at the same time. "You goddamn son-of-a-bitch, you're the best friend I ever had."

Now why doesn't alcohol help put us in touch with our real feelings? Why aren't rage and self-pity healthy? They're emotions, after all. They break the pattern of control we have been living by.

This is complicated, and I'm not sure I understand it fully. But here's what I think.

Alcohol doesn't help, and rage and self-pity don't relieve us of our pain, because what they express is our *false* self, not our true one. It's our false self, after all, that's trying to hide from our real anger. It's our false self that denies our grief and pain.

So alcoholics like my dad can get drunk night after night, armoring themselves in their false self, and wake up every morning with that false self broken to pieces, and have to seek the security of their addiction to rebuild the false self, and never come into touch with their real self.

That's sad, isn't it? I mean, is it because I'm just an adult child of an alcoholic that I think it's sad?

My poor father, who in some ways I love more than anybody in the world — you see? He's screwed me up in just the way he is! — my poor father can't *get* to himself as long as he drinks. Because he spends all his energy propping up his false self — the self that says everything's fine in his life and everyone loves old Jimmy Lee, because he always has a tear and a dollar for the crippled woman on the street corner and a smile for everyone.

Arggh!!!

(Sighs.)

I am getting real steamed and real sad talking about my dad. And the energy in here is getting a bit intense.

Get up!

Let's move! Everybody move your arms around. Shake your bodies.

Move it! Move it! Move it!

(Audience laughs. Sounds of commotion.)

Keep stirring around. That looks real nice.

Next time I'll bring music and we'll have a dance.

And none of those old ballroom dances — you know, where you have a ramrod up your rear. Nosiree. *Funky* down-home dances with lots of bending and shaking.

Used to be, I couldn't dance without two or three beers. Give me beer, and this boy was Fred Astaire.

Well, part of my recovery now is being able to dance like a fool *cold sober! (Audience laughs.)*

Is that enough?

(Audience comments.)

Okay, don't let me interrupt. Anytime you want to get up and dance at one of my talks, feel free.

Whew. Maybe we ought to combine with a jazzercise class.

Okay. I want to talk about what just happened.

I had strong feelings come up about my dad, and I didn't want to stifle them. I wanted to let them out. This was an appropriate place to do it because I knew you wouldn't be hurt by whatever I felt about my dad.

I do thank you all for letting me express what I felt.

Now if I had been angry with *you* — if you were my girlfriend, say, or a colleague at work — then it might not have been appropriate for me to express my feelings to you. Not till I'd checked out that the feelings were really called up by what was going on now in our relationship.

I'll be talking about this later — how we check where our feelings come from and how we express them appropriately.

For now, we've still got to answer the question, "What do we do with anger and grief?"

Well, we don't do what we usually do — that's for damn sure.

We don't *deny* our feelings. We don't *bury* them. We don't numb them down with TV, food, sex and work.

We don't medicate them away with drugs, legal or illegal. We don't *meditate* them away or "transcend" them or "turn them over" before we've experienced them.

We don't mask them under depression or behind a smile.

I had a woman in a group session today who said that when she was five she walked into the living room and her mother kicked her in the stomach. She said that with a smile.

Do you find yourself telling stuff that's deeply painful with a smile on your face? What does the smile say?

It says: "I don't want anyone to take this seriously, most of all me."

It says: "If I smile, I minimize the pain I'm feeling — or I seem to. So I protect me and my mother."

Your mamma doesn't need protection. She's a big girl. You can kick her in the stomach, verbally — it's your turn. Or name a pillow after her and punch her out good.

Just imagine the energy it took that woman to tell what she told *and smile.*

Most of us have so much anger and sadness in us that we spend anywhere from 20 to 80 percent of our disposable energy just keeping them in. And then we wonder why we're tired at the end of the day. Why we weren't more productive at the end of the year.

You women have a special problem. A few of you men, too, but mainly you women. Men come to you expecting you to take care of their anger and pain. Suffer it for them. Show them how to handle it.

You all know why this is. Our fathers weren't taught how to deal with their emotions. They were told that men held their feelings in, just like frozen-puss John Wayne and Robert Mitchum.

You know, they had Mitchum star in that miniseries on World War II because they said he was one of the few actors from the time still alive.

How did they know? (Audience laughs.) I mean, did they *look* at him? All he shows is rigor mortis.

So boys come to rely on their mothers to handle their emotions and set their example. And when we boys grow up, we still rely on women. If we're feeling pain or grief or anger, or sometimes if we're feeling real joy — anything we're uneasy with — we come and *dump* it on a woman.

"I have pain. You have mammary glands. Mamma had mammary glands. You are Mamma — or near enough."

You women have to protect yourself. You have to say, "Get that messy greasy kid stuff away from me, Buster. That's yours! You take care of it yourself."

Because nobody can do somebody else's emotional work for them.

Another thing. We've got to treat our anger *as* anger. Anger being so dangerous, we keep disguising it. We turn it into *passive* aggression. Instead of telling a subordinate the work he's doing is unacceptable, we shake our head and say, "You just can't do any better, can you?"

Ooo, that smarts!

When my old girlfriend Laurel and I had a fight, she got over it right away — which pissed me off royally. *(Audience laughs.)*

The reason she got over it was that she knew how to express her feelings. She'd take this big purse she had and throw it against the wall, shouting, "I'm fucking furious!" Wham! the room would shake.

And you know, like a kid who throws a tantrum, it got the anger out. Ten minutes later she'd be in the kitchen whistling and peeling vegetables. Me, I'd be in the bedroom, trying to meditate away my anger, my stomach twisted in 55 knots.

After a while she'd say, "Supper's ready!"

And I'd say, "I can't eat. My stomach's all knotted up."

And she'd say, "Are you *still* angry?"

And I'd say — this was back when I was prematurely nice — "Now I've told you, sweetheart, I don't get angry. Please don't accuse me of that. Now I'm going to have to meditate some more." *(Audience laughs.)*

Okay. So a month goes by. I'm still steaming. We're invited to a party, and Laurel takes four hours getting ready. Tries on every dress. She comes out looking great, 30 minutes late as usual.

And I look up and say to her, "Oh . . . Are you going to wear that?"

Bam!

Wiped out! Crushed! DOA! *(Audience laughs.)*

Chalk up another win for passive-aggression!

But in the long run it was a loss. She knew enough to leave me because of stunts like that.

Let your anger be healthy, clean anger. Not manipulation. Not subterfuge. Not tears.

You've seen that happen — somebody's really angry but they start crying. It's like they can't *stay* in their anger.

Now there are several reasons for this. Many women can't stay in their anger because they learned nice girls don't get angry. Nice girls eat their anger. Nice boys do too. They douse the fire of their anger with tears, because tears were more acceptable in their family of origin.

Thank heavens for nice girls and boys. Without them, three-quarters of us therapists would go broke.

Women often turn their anger to tears because they can't afford to get as angry as they feel. If they did, they'd kick their husband out of the house and be left with the kids and the bills. They cry because crying doesn't cut them off from him as much as anger would.

And there is another reason people cry. They cry because they can't *reach* their anger. They weren't allowed to as children and now the way is blocked. They cry in frustration. Their real self is cut off from them.

Frustrated people often say the person they're really angry at is themselves. "I keep making the same dumb mistakes in my relationships." "I'm the most godawful co-dependent in the world." "I've got nobody to blame but myself."

Now this kind of talk is wrong, self-pitying and dangerous.

It's wrong because you certainly do have someone else to blame — whoever taught you the unhealthy patterns you're living by. Do you think I became an alcoholic and learned how to ruin relationships with women all by myself? Nope. My dad was there long before me. And my mom's dad before him.

I need to be appropriately angry at the people and conditions that caused my problem, not only at me.

Now, granted, to set things right, I have to take responsibility for things being wrong. But I mustn't punish myself by thinking that everything's my fault. If I do, guilt and self-pity could immobilize me.

That's the danger when anger is pointed inward at the self — that the self will wilt under the assault. Anger should make us stronger, but if we point it inward it can weaken us.

Now listen closely. I'm going to say this plainly, but you're not going to tell anybody I said it because it sounds a little mystical.

Your emotions . . . my emotions . . . his emotions . . . her emotions don't entirely belong to us. They're not supposed to. They are prompted by things outside us, and we are supposed to express them outside us.

When an emotion comes up in us, what we are meant to do is feel it just as deeply as we can for as long as it works upon us. Then let it go. Express it — literally, push it out — into the universe where it came from.

Trouble starts when we try to keep a negative feeling in us. If we internalize *anger*, how can we forgive ourselves? If we internalize *fear*, how can we trust the world? If we internalize *grief*, what sweetness is there in living?

Feelings aren't supposed to get stuck in us.

But before we can let a feeling go, we have to experience it. And to do this, we have to get in touch with it and feel it.

Now if we can't do this, we need help. We need a safe person and a safe place to work on our feelings — do what I call emotional release work.

I'd like to say that any therapist you go to will be able to help, but this isn't true. Most therapists don't know how to deal with deep anger and deep grief. You say, "I'm sad," and the therapist says, "Yes? Tell me about it." And you go straight to your head, rather than to the grief that's in your body.

It's even worse with anger. Just look at the therapist's counseling room. Smooth desk, pictures, fancy chairs, flowers in breakable vases. You're paying for all that in more ways than one. That's a room people aren't supposed to get angry in.

I went to a therapist who was very good, but she didn't allow anger. She did allow grief, which helped me a lot. She allowed grief because she'd been through grief herself and knew how much it counted. So I could cry and cry without having to intellectualize it.

Which is just what you want to do.

You want to do with your anger and grief what you do with all your feelings. Feel them — feel them as much as you can. *Experience* them. Then, when you're done, express them and let them pass from you into the world.

When a feeling comes up again, you do the same thing again.

You get rid of your repressed anger and grief the same way you piled them in your closet: one layer at a time.

Or let's change the metaphor. Instead of a closet, let's make your stockpile of feelings a well. You empty the well the same way it fills: drop by drop, dipper by dipper.

Do you ever get to the bottom?

I know I haven't. And I don't know how you'd know if you did. But you reduce the contents and their pressure in you.

Now to do this takes time and patience. And adult children from dysfunctional families aren't patient. Oh, we can *wait* forever — but we haven't any patience, right?

We want a quick fix. We want a pill that will make our grief and anger go away — snap! like *that.* We want a spiritual path that will — I think I got this quote from a New Age journal — "burn our negativity in the white light of the heart chakra." *(Audience laughs.)*

Ahhh! Burn me, baby!

If it works for you, that's great. It doesn't work for me.

The pain was laid in one layer at a time since we were three, four, five. I believe it's got to come out the same way.

This is why I favor the Gestalt method of re-experiencing feeling to close old wounds and Bio-energetics to discharge the body's blocked energy.

Let me give you an example of what I mean.

I want a volunteer who's real angry about something. Any-body who —

(A woman has immediately stood up.)

Why, thank you. I have the impression maybe you've been waiting for this chance. Stockpiling your anger.

Come on up.

Do you want to tell us what you're angry about?

Woman: No.

John: No? Well, that's okay. We don't want to know. Except we're curious. *(Audience laughs.)*

You *are* angry?

Woman: Yes.

John: You promise? Cross your heart? You're just repressing it real hard, so you appear calm? *(Audience laughs.)*

Woman: I'm angry.

John: That's fine. Now I want you to take this towel in both hands and think about what you're so angry about. And as you keep thinking about it, I want you to twist the towel as hard as you can. Twist it until your body says it's had enough.

(The woman twists the towel.)

Whew! I see you *are* angry. *(Audience laughs.)*

(The woman says something.)
John: What?
Woman: Can I close my eyes?
John: Can you — ? Sure!
(The woman twists the towel some more. Audience laughs. Applause.)
Well, thank you very much. That was wonderful.
How do you feel?
Woman: I feel good. Real good.
John: Well, you sure did a job on my towel. *(Audience laughs.)*
You see all the twists in the towel — that's where you put your feeling, instead of twisting up your stomach or your shoulders.
You expressed your anger, and nobody got hurt, right?
Woman: Not me.
John: No, and not the audience. Nobody's hurt.
Do you feel you have more energy?
Woman: You want me to twist another towel? *(Audience laughs.)*
John: She's got energy!
Thank you very much.
(John and the woman embrace. Audience applauds. The woman returns to her chair.)

So the equation we grew up with — anger equals pain — isn't always true. Anger expressed appropriately will bring peace and increased energy and well-being.

But let me say again what I mean to say in every talk. The way to your feelings is through your body. That's the only place you feel. So, to heal your spirit, you have to start with your body.

One time I had a client, a man of 46. When he was nine, he saw his father go after his mother with a carving knife. Ever after, he was deeply angry to have watched his father do that and been too small to do anything about it. He was angry mainly at himself. He shouldn't have been, but *telling* him this didn't do any good.

I said to him, "Paul, what did you want to do then — when you saw your dad with the knife?"

He said, "I wanted to grab my dad's wrist and make him drop it."

As he said those words, his hands moved in the air — they sort of darted up — and he leaned forward in the chair.

He had been wanting to *do* something for 37 years. He'd been replaying and replaying in his mind the scene that fueled his anger, but he had never expressed it in his body.

So I suggested we do some psychodrama. I played the dad. I pretended I had a knife, and he went for my wrist and we wrestled as hard as we could, our arms locked together. He was grunting and cursing, till I saw he was completely engaged and I let go.

Right away his body relaxed, and he fell on the floor. He was breathing heavily and so was I. Then, to my surprise, he started laughing. He lay there on the floor and laughed and laughed.

When he was over the conniptions, I said, "Paul, what in God's name was so funny?"

That set him off again! *(Audience laughs.)* And me, too.

Well, he told me everything was fine. He had finally got the pain out. He was laughing because he felt so *light*. So free.

He said it had seemed a stupid thing to do, the psychodrama, and here it had made him feel so different. He was laughing about that, too.

When people do anger or grief work, their face gets lighter. Look at somebody after they've had a good cry. Their face is relaxed, and there's a lot of sparkle in their eyes.

Now it's interesting that our culture likes men *not* to have that sparkle. You know, be like Robert Mitchum.

Tall, dark, and handsome — that's the phrase. And the darkness is not skin tone. It's moodiness. Sadness. Pain internalized so it clouds the countenance.

Marlon Brando. Jimmy Dean. Robert DeNiro. Mick Jagger. Humphrey Bogart. Al Pacino. Montgomery Clift. I've played them all. Trying to impress women.

We need some healthier heroes, that's what it comes down to. We need some men who can surrender their pain and accept joy.

I want to tell you about one more psychodrama. This was a couple who had been fighting for three days, so they came to see me. I draw some pretty special types.

They may have known what began their fight, but they couldn't say it in a way I understood. Jill gave a tirade, then Jim did. They were mad as hell.

I said, "How would you describe your current relationship?"

And Jill said, "What a dumb-shit question! We're fighting like cats and dogs!"

I said, "Jim which are you — cat or dog?"

Jim said, "Well, I've always liked dog."

Jill said, "And *I love cats!*" *(Audience laughs.)*

So I said, "Let's fight it out then. I want you down on all fours. Jim, you bark and growl — no biting. Jill, you hiss and spit — no scratching."

Now my office used to be in my home, and my neighbors heard all kinds of things, but this was the first time they were tempted to call the ASPCA. *(Audience laughs.)* For the rest of the session Jim and Jill went at it — barking and hissing, clawing the air, making moves to bite, chasing and dodging. Not a word spoken.

At the end of 20 minutes, they were laughing like crazy. They embraced each other, and the fight was over. Their anger was spent.

Now what made them better? What made Paul better — the man whose father had taken a knife to his mother? What, if I'm right, made our friend here better when she twisted the towel?

I think what made them better was that for a moment they were able to lose control. *Safely.*

In order to heal, we have to break down the defenses we've put up and feel what we've been hiding from. Come into contact with our real self. And the only way to do it is to lose control.

Now because we're children of dysfunctional families we fear the loss of control more than anything. We grew up in situations where there wasn't any healthy control, so we decided about age six that we had to rule the universe. *(Audience laughs.)* Well, someone with sense had to do it.

But if we're always in control, magic can't happen to us.

The child says, "Mamma, this is the most beautiful rock ever, ever. Look at those sparkles."

The child is in the magic moment. The child has given control over to the universe, knowing that the universe has endless wonders to show.

If we can't surrender control, we can't see the wonders.

If we can't surrender control, we can't learn to swim — because we fear the water too much.

We can't ride a bicycle — because we fear falling.

We can't fall asleep — because we fear helplessness.

We can't see God in a handful of flowers.

We can't let ourselves have an orgasm.

We can't dance.

We can't cry.

We can't feel.

We can't die.

The Austin paper had an article the other week about a painter, Geoffrey Graham, a gay man who is dying of AIDS. And he said something so beautiful I wrote it down.

(Reads.) "I have no fear of death. It's a natural part of life. I trust the universe enough not to be fearful."

He's surrendered control.

Now we've tried to recapture the uncontrolled, magic moments we knew as children through drugs and alcohol and sex and food. We've used prayer and meditation. And these things have given us little bits of the magic.

My belief is we can get the magic better if we learn to open ourselves to our feelings, as my cat-and-dog clients did. As our friend here did with the towel. As Geoffrey Graham did.

When we open ourselves, for a second or two we forget what's around us — just don't care who's watching — and lose control and the need for control. The cries and howls and pain and joy and ecstasy and laughter come up, take us over and pass through us into the universe.

But *safely.* This loss of control isn't like rage or self-pity — it's safe. All the while Jim and Jill were playing cats and dogs, they were Jim and Jill. They knew not to bite or scratch. The whole time we fought, Paul knew he wasn't fighting with his father. All the time our friend was twisting her anger into the towel, she knew what she was doing and would have told us if we had called her out of her emotion.

So it's not like alcohol or drugs or meditation.

We lose control, but we don't lose control.

And we come back from it with the charge gone from our emotions. It's passed back into the universe. Now our anger is clean. We can say "I'm angry" or "I was angry" without frightening other people. Or ourselves.

If we need to, after we say "I'm angry," we can add that dangerous word *because*. "I'm angry because we agreed to meet at seven." The person we're speaking to will hear that and understand that our anger comes only from the present event, without a layer of past anger.

The funny thing is, having lost control to get in touch with our feelings, we now have our feelings under control.

The two sets of feelings are different, of course. One is the dirty mound of childhood feelings in our closet. The other is small, clean anger growing out of what's just happened.

So, okay — what do we do with our anger and grief?

First, we feel them. Just as hard and deeply as we can. This sometimes means we have to withdraw from other people. It may mean getting with a safe person to talk to. Someone who will support us, give us reassuring hugs if we need them.

Second, if our feeling is bigger than makes sense, given the event that triggered it, we've got to get in touch with the feelings in our closet, feel them and let them pass.

Third, once the old feelings are over, we return to the world and state flatly what we feel. "I'm sad." "I'm angry." "I feel hurt." Often we don't have to say why — the other person will understand or accept our feeling without knowing the cause. "I was feeling real angry just then, but it's over." "I have a pain in my stomach, so I don't want to talk about this now." "I'm feeling much better, and I'm ready to discuss things with you."

If we have to make a negative judgment on someone, we do it flatly, without demeaning them. "I'm sorry, this isn't working, and I am going to make some changes." "I've decided not to reappoint you. You see the job one way, I see it another. I want to work with someone else." "We've had a good time as lovers. I hope we'll have a good time as friends. I'm very sad to do this, but I want out and I'm getting out."

The frightening passions of anger and grief can be made safe — or anyhow a lot safer.

Now I know some of you have been needing a restroom for a number of minutes and been too polite to say so. *(Audience laughs.)*

You're free! That's it!

Thank you very much for your attention. Fifteen-minute break, and then I hope you'll come back and say what's on your mind.

Healing Co-dependency
And Depression
Through Movement,
Sounds And Silence

I want to welcome you here tonight — those of you who want to be here and the rest of you.

Actually, I'm one person who's looking forward to this talk because I haven't heard it before.

Something went wrong with those jokes. You were supposed to laugh. *(Audience laughs.)*

Yep, this is a new talk. It would have been part of the series on co-dependency I gave last spring, except these ideas came to me too late.

Now I'm going to assume we all know what co-dependency is. You remember: co-dependency is a disease suffered by a person who depends on someone else or something else to make him or her feel better.

We all know what depression is, unfortunately. Let me remind you that it *isn't* sadness. Sadness is an emotion and depression is an absence of emotion, a *suppression* of emotion.

Okay. I've come to believe that co-dependency and depression are two sides of the same coin. A co-dependent person is usually a depressed person, for reasons I'll explain in a second.

I'm a co-dependent, and before I got into recovery I was depressed most of the time. Up until three or four years ago, I was depressed 85 percent of the time. In a good week.

How many of you are depressed a lot of the time?

You see? You're so depressed you won't raise your hands. *(Audience laughs.)*

Still, that's nearly a third of the audience.

Oop! there's some more hands. A burst of movement. Thank you.

Now why are co-dependents so likely to be depressed?

Co-dependents want the world to reward them for playing the false-self role their parents taught them to play. Playing that role, they suppress whatever their real self is — or *was*, since it was crushed long ago.

Playing their false self, they swallow their real feelings and sit on them. They use a good part of their energy keeping down what they feel.

Thus, (1) their *energy* is depressed and (2) they don't know what they feel — so *they* are depressed.

That's pretty clear, huh? A co-dependent can't help but be depressed some of the time.

Now, if I had spoken to you this afternoon and said, "Tell me the truth. How do you feel about going to that talk of mine tonight?" you might have answered, "Well, John, frankly, it depresses the shit out of me."

And I would have said, "Me too! And I have to stay awake the whole time."

But then I would have said, "Let's work on that depression of yours. What's underneath it?"

We would have talked about your past and childhood until a feeling came up in you. Because under every depression there is a stifled feeling.

I'm willing to bet your feeling about coming here tonight would be either anger or sadness.

I know when I get depressed about going to a talk like this or to a 12-Step meeting, the feeling I'm covering up is anger. It's *rage*. I'm totally pissed off that I have to do therapy! I'd so much rather spend my time and money on something else. But I have to go to lectures and meetings and counseling because I'm an adult child of my parents. I mean, for all the good they did me I might as well have been raised by two vacant lots.

You see? Rip off the depression and you find some honest anger under it. Or sadness. Or fear.

So here's one thing I didn't understand when I gave those talks on co-dependency last spring: As we recover from co-dependency, we're likely at the same time to recover from depression.

Two for the price of one, huh? Good deal.

All right. Tonight I'm going to give you three ways of re-covering from co-dependency and depression. As the title says, "Through Movement, Sounds and Silence." I like that phrase.

You must like it too — it brought you here tonight. Now let's see if it means anything.

One thing you hear co-dependents say all the time is, "I'm stuck. I do the same old things, day after day, in my job and my relationships. I'm not getting anywhere. I just repeat the same patterns. I'm not changing — I'm stuck in one place."

I would guess that many of you feel this way about your lives or you wouldn't be here, looking to change. I know I felt a little bit stuck giving the same lectures again and again. That's why I decided to try something new tonight.

Adult children of dysfunctional families like us are always going to be falling into stuckness, getting glued into our patterns, because we hunger so much for consistency and control. We're so fearful of being abandoned.

What can we do to keep from being stuck?

Well, we can *move*.

Pretty simple, eh?

Now I'm not talking about moving to Oregon, though that wouldn't be bad. I'd like to see rain again before I die.

And I'm not talking about moving back home to our par-ents, God forbid! Some of us, when we get really stuck and really depressed, start thinking about that. We call Mom and Dad and say, "Mom and Dad, I'm going through a real rough patch. *(Sniffle, sniffle.)* Yeah, money would help, but actually what I was thinking was, you know how you always wish I could pay a longer visit . . . ?" *(Audience laughs.)*

Maybe they've kept your bed warm, with Rubber Ducky in the bath.

Of course you understand that part of your wanting to move back is disguised anger and aggression. You want to show your parents how they failed to bring you up so you could take care of yourself. "You didn't support me as a baby. By God you're going to support me as an adult!"

What I'm talking about now, though, is *healthy* movement.

Let's say you wake up in the morning so depressed you can't even get out of bed. You know the way that is? Your highest aspiration is to raise yourself up and hobble over to the desk and write in your diary, "October 8, 1989. Depressed." *(Audience laughs.)*

But you can't even do that. You're too depressed.

Fact is, if you could start writing in your diary, that'd be a way of getting you moving. It might help you discover what was causing the feelings you were hiding from yourself.

But you can't get out of bed! You're lying there waiting for someone to rush in the room and save you. Mom and Dad! The Kemper Cavalry! You're praying to the telephone, "Ring, you bastard, and change my life!" *(Audience laughs.)*

Now I'm the last person to say there's anything wrong with prayer. It's an important part of recovery. But a co-dependent's prayers go like this: *(Teary)* "Dear God, I'm depressed. Please do something about it. Bring somebody half-decent into my life. Give me a good job. Or kill my boss. *(Audience laughs.)* If I had a good job and somebody to love me, I'd feel great, Lord. I promise I would."

Boo-hoo-hoo.

About six months ago I woke up depressed. I got up and went to the bathroom and got back into bed. I pulled the covers over my head. I thought, "Wow! I haven't done this in years. Boy, this is the example I use in my lecture about being depressed. You pull the cover over your head and want the morning to go away."

I threw the covers off, leaped out of bed, ran to my counseling room and started beating the crap out of every pillow
I could find. I threw things and jumped and stomped and
screamed "I don't want to be depressed!" and cursed and
flung myself around. Finally, after maybe five minutes, I started crying. Completely broke down. Sobbing.

Then I realized I'd been suppressing anger and sadness
about a couple of things that were going on in my life. I
don't even remember now what they were. Having realized
this, I started laughing at what a wild man I'd been and how
good it felt and what a mess I'd made — one of the pillows
had broken and I had little pellets of foam rubber all over
the room.

When you start moving, really moving, your feelings come
up fast.

Needless to say, when you're depressed, the last thing you
want to do is exercise. But every time you go on and do it
anyhow, you'll feel better. Every time.

Your movement has got to be physical. Screaming, yelling,
pounding, shaking, kicking, crying, throwing, dancing, walking, running, biking, wrestling, sawing, riding. This is particularly true for people who weren't allowed to express their
anger physically as children — you know, in temper tantrums,
as we call them.

Now movement that's healthy doesn't have to be so vigor-
ous. Writing, as I say, can do the trick. Or talking: When you
wake up depressed, pick up the phone and call a supportive
friend and talk about how you feel. That's movement.

There's got to be movement. If you spend all your time
reading good books on recovery, forget it — you won't get
better. My mother prayed for my father to stop being an alcoholic for 37 years. All that while she also prayed to be content
in her life. It didn't work. He numbed himself with drink, and
she numbed herself with Valium and prayer.

To change things, she had to stand up and say, "Enough. No
more," and leave the house and go to Al-Anon. Then she had
to tell my father what her needs were. When he couldn't meet
them, she had to tell him to move out.

Now some of you will remember that when I spoke about co-dependency last spring, I mentioned the importance of breaking patterns. That's what I'm talking about here. Shaking things up. Moving against your patterns.

Your heaviest pattern is pleasing other people. Move against it. Move away from pleasing others — your mom and dad, your spouse, your boss, your children — and see what happens.

At age 35, 45, 60, some of us are still in jobs and relationships and geographical locales because they pleased our parents. Who may be dead by then!

"I'm staying here in Oshkosh because Mamma loved it so. She'd want me to be here."

Half the people in this room aren't doing what they really want to in life. And I'm not so sure about the *other* half! *(Audience laughs.)*

That's because their father told them, "Son, do this." Or their mother, "Honey, we'd be real proud of you." The parents told the daughter, "He's a good man. He'll make a dependable husband. You can't do better, plain as you are."

I remember asking a college student one time — a great big husky fellow — what he was going to do.

He said, "I'm going to be an accountant."

I said, "You've got to be kidding. You can't add two and two. What gives you the idea of being an accountant?"

"My dad's an accountant," he said. "I'm going to be an accountant."

I asked if that was what he wanted. We talked for a few minutes, and tears ran down his cheeks.

"If my dad would get off my back and say it was okay whatever I did, I'd try to be a forest ranger," he said. "Or in conservation. Something outdoors."

Last I knew, that boy was becoming an accountant.

When you move against pleasing the people who matter most in your life, you open yourself to the unknown. Mystery! Adventure! Danger! You don't know what those people are going to say.

Did you know, if you stop pleasing Mom and Dad, they may stop speaking to you?

Someone says, "Jesus Christ! Why didn't I know that before? *(Audience laughs.)* I've been trying to get them to stop calling me for 15 years, and you tell me all I have to do is stop pleasing them. Hallelujah, I'm free!"

You can be — if you're willing to be. Co-dependents are scared to death of being abandoned. But if you beat that fear, you beat co-dependency.

Okay. Physical movement. Movement against your patterns. Movement against pleasing others. Is this making sense so far?

I hope it is. I'm such a damned co-dependent I need you all to get this. *(Audience laughs.)*

You know, I can't fix a car, I don't understand computers, I'm a lousy cook, I couldn't write a dissertation. So if I can't give a clear talk, I'm in trouble. My dad will say, "See? I told you to get a real job!"

So you've got to follow me, hear?

Now I'm going to talk about something embarrassing, and I want to apologize ahead of time. I'm going to talk about masturbation.

That casts a chill in the room. *(Audience laughs.)*

People like *doing* it — we just don't like talking about it.

I haven't mentioned it in a talk before, but I have to here because I'm talking about movement as a way of overcoming co-dependency and depression. I know it's going to take me a little while to get started on this topic, so I ask you to be patient with me for a minute. Of course, speak up if anything I say is unclear.

All right.

We all have needs. Food, shelter, companionship, intimacy, etc. Most of us have a need for sexual release.

Now if your needs for intimacy and touching are being met — that's a big *if* — but if they are, then masturbation is a way of meeting your sexual need that can keep you from making risky, unwise, co-dependent commitments.

I say this because I know I've gotten myself involved with lots of women I regretted ever knowing just because I wanted to screw them.

You think ahead of time, when the sexual need is strong in you, that screwing this woman or that woman — hell, *any* woman, however unsuitable or damaged — would be much more fun than getting sexual release by yourself, through masturbating.

But that's *before* you do the deed. *(Audience laughs.) After* you've screwed the woman, if she's clinging or gullible or mean or needy — as she almost certainly is — I guarantee you're going to wish you'd masturbated. You're going to lie there in bed wishing she'd drop off the earth.

If instead of screwing the woman or man, you had masturbated, afterwards you'd be glad. You'd think, "How could I have been so hot to trot I wanted to take *that person* to bed?"

I said that masturbation was healthy so long as your needs for intimacy and touching were being met. If those needs aren't being met, then masturbation can become just another addiction — a way to numb out the pain of being unable to give and receive intimacy.

We're a very genitally focused culture, so it's important to make clear that the needs for intimacy and touching and affection can all be met without sexual union.

Intimacy happens when one person reveals something private about himself or herself in the expectation that another person will empathize and maybe reciprocate. We can be intimate with countless people, and I don't see why we shouldn't. I'm all for promiscuous intimacy! *(Audience laughs.)* As you can tell, listening to me talk about masturbation.

There are many kinds of touching, but the most important, I think, is the hug. Because it shows that the whole person is accepted, *valued* by somebody else.

Nowadays, thanks to the men's movement, it's okay for men to hug one another, and that's a wonderful thing.

So here's the bottom line: You can get your needs for touching and intimacy met without going to bed with someone. If you need a heart-to-heart talk, seek out a friend, someone you know is safe. If you need a hug, ask for it.

Any of you — male or female — who needs hugs or intimate talk, you've got an invitation to the Austin Men's Center, 1611

West Sixth Street, a safe place for men, women and children. Come in to see us, say you need a hug and we'll give you one.

As for your sex needs, we won't help. *(Audience laughs.)* You can handle that yourself.

All right, enough about movement. Now sounds.

(John consults notes. Pause.)

This part of the lecture is a little weird, too. *(Laughs.)* I thought once we got beyond masturbation we were home free.

I'm going to tell you three things I believe and most therapists don't. First, your past is recorded in your body. Second, a co-dependent's body is full of the pain of his or her childhood. Third, the *sounds* of your past and your pain have to come out for you to heal.

Most therapy is head-centered. Now the head matters because the head understands. But the body matters too, because it's the body that *feels* and, through feeling, remembers. The word *remembers* has the body in it, you know; the body's *members* are what remembers.

To recover we have to rid our body of bad feelings and memories.

Okay. That's clear but pretty abstract.

To make it more concrete, I'm going to do what I usually do: talk about me. When I tell you my ideas, it's just head stuff. When I tell my *story,* I go back into my body, and you can feel what I mean.

When I was a kid, I wanted to go into my mom and dad's room and say, "Stop it! Stop fighting! Please, stop arguing. Stop hurting each other." But of course I couldn't.

So there are a thousand *stop its* still in my body.

And all those times I wanted to say, "No more, Dad. Please don't." They're still there.

I've got lots of them out, but I can tell from talking about it now that they're not all out. That's the thing about recovery work: It takes the rest of your life, as the pain comes up.

I have countless cries and sighs and screams and shouts and moans and *no's* and *go away's* and *leave me alone's* and *don't hit her's* and *don't drink's* and *please stay with me's* and *let's love each other before we grow up and die's* still in my body.

I expect they are in yours, too, from the way some of you
look.

Now those sounds need to come out. That's what my therapy and workshops mainly do: Encourage people to let their
bodies speak. Scream. Shout. Weep. Moan. Sigh.

Deep sighs. *(Sighs.)*

Just *that* lets out some pain and tension. Sighing is very
good for you.

I wonder if I'm the only one here who was ordered not to
sigh as a child. I'd come in the house, see what was going on
and let out a sigh to calm myself and give me strength.

"*Stop that sighing,* young man!" Mom or Dad would shout.

I never understood why. It was impolite or something.

Any of the rest of you told not to sigh?

Yeah, you see? Amazing.

So you've got lots of sighs to get out. And moans. And great
big wrenching sobs.

People usually cry in a pussyfooting stifled way, holding it
in because they don't want to disturb others. But you need to
cry full out. Cry to your depths.

Preferably, you need to do this emotional release work with
other people — *safe* people, in safe circumstances.

I'll tell you why. Two reasons. One, you were hurt among
other people, so you need to heal among them. Two, you
need to learn to express your true feelings with other people,
as you weren't allowed to do with your parents. When it's
done with others, emotional release work is both a healing
and a learning experience.

But you can do a lot of healing by yourself. You can get in
your car and scream, "I hate you, you son-of-a-bitch!" 15 times
at the top of your lungs — you know, talking to your boss or
your husband or whoever — and feel a lot better.

Once you start letting the painful sounds out, you'll find
you have room to let in the peaceful sounds of the earth. The
birds and crickets and wind and rain. Sounds we almost never
listen to because we're so tense and busy and hurt.

You'll find you have room to take in new experiences, and
thus change and grow. If you hold in your anger at your
parents, repress it because it scares you, then your whole

system freezes, gets stuck. You've got to *let go* to *take in.* It's a paradox.

Right. Talking about sounds leads me to silence.

Once you let out the painful sounds clogging your body, you'll be able to hear silence for the first time and hear very quiet sounds, like the child's voice within you.

The child in you is trying to tell you what you need to know, and if you get silent enough, you'll hear.

That child in us got squelched when we were small. God, didn't it! I was watching a little girl the other day with her daddy. She was about two years old and had this rock big as her fist. She said, "Look Daddy. Boo-tiful rock. Boo-tiful, boo-tiful."

And he said, "Put that dirty thing down! You're getting mud all over."

Squash. The magic and mystery of rocks just went down the drain. The girl dropped the rock.

Somewhere far down in us we still have that child's voice. You don't know what you want to do with your life? You don't know whether to get married? If you could remove the pain from your body and get quiet enough, your voice would tell you. It knows everything you need to know.

Now some people tell me, "Aw, you're just idealizing the child."

You're damn right I am! *(Audience laughs.)*

That child deserves to be idealized — just as we did when we were children.

Anybody who says I'm idealizing the child is really saying, "I didn't get idealized as a child, and I don't want you to do it in front of me."

We've got to be big enough, when we've admitted our pain and felt it deep as we can, to let it pass from us. Not to hang on to it by envying people who don't share it.

I remember during the Vietnam War there was this mother from Bronxville, New York. Her son was drafted and killed, and after that she became a leader in the anti-war movement. She said something like "Just because my son was killed doesn't mean other mothers have to lose their sons."

(Sighs.) Yeah. Pretty amazing.

She had let go of her pain. She didn't insist that everybody feel it.

Just because I had a miserable childhood, I don't insist that other people suffer. That's what Alice Miller says Hitler did. In her book *For Your Own Good* she says Hitler grew up believing the violence practiced on him as a child was *right,* he identified with his abuser, and so he practiced violence on everyone he could.

I like to think we can break this pattern of victim-become-victimizer by deciding to give our children good childhoods, regardless of the childhood we had ourselves. I hope that a generation or two or three from now people will be better, happier than we are, because they will have learned how to raise children. I think we're beginning to learn.

One way to learn is to listen to that child in you. Listen with respect. Listen with love. It will teach you.

Even at my worst, when I was drinking and doing drugs and screwing anything that moved, even then I could sometimes hear my inner child. I always knew it was sacred. It saved me from total despair. I'd think, "If only I could get to that voice!"

And I'd take some more bourbon or pot. Or I'd meditate six hours at a clip, until I couldn't see straight.

Even then I was telling my friends, "Listen to your inner voice."

And most of them slapped me on the back and said, "Yeah, man, fucking A!" *(Audience laughs.)*

Whatever the hell that meant. *(Laughs.)*

But Laurel listened to me — the woman I tell about loving in my book *The Flying Boy.* One day about four years ago she told me she was leaving.

I asked why.

"John," she said, "you didn't give me much. You didn't teach me much. But one thing you showed me was to look for the voice inside me, and listen to it."

"Yeah?" I said.

"The voice told me it's time to leave."

"Oh, *that* voice," I said. "Don't listen to that! That's not the voice I was talking about." *(Audience laughs.)*

We both got a good laugh out of that.

She listened to her inner voice. There's no memory of her I cherish more than her telling me that.

The only way to get to the voice, once you've overcome fear and co-dependency, is through silence.

A way to move toward silence, and toward healing your co-dependency and depression too, is by deep breathing and listening to your breathing.

Most people know something about this, but they forget to breathe. Especially when they're depressed and under stress and co-dependent.

You want to know how you're feeling? Check your breathing. If you're breathing full, deep, filling breaths, I almost guarantee that you're in good shape. If you're breathing from your throat, you're scared. "What's he going to do next?" "How's she going to hurt me?" "What will she say?" "Has he got a knife?"

Your breathing is shallow because your body is in a state of contraction. Timid. Defensive. Frozen.

Deep breathing, big sighs — those are first steps to health and silence.

Another way to silence is by shutting up. *(Laughs.)*

Many of us talk when we're scared. Some of us lecture — like me! I used to be the world's worst. Somebody could be talking to me, trying to be intimate. I'd get scared and — pop! — start to lecture.

They'd say, "I just need you to hold me, or hug me, or listen to me."

And I'd say, "You sound awful co-dependent to me. *(Audience laughs.)* Do you know that's a real disease? I wrote a book on it. Sold lots of copies. And there are other books too. I'll make a list."

Silence. It's real comforting.

When you're feeling needy, when old pain is coming up, when your spouse or boss or parents or kids are pushing your butt, just say, "Okay. Let's not talk about this right now." And go off to work on your feelings.

I hear you shouting, all together, "That's avoiding the issue!" *(Audience laughs.)*

Maybe. For a while. Because you're dealing with a more basic issue.

When you surround yourself with silence, you build boundaries. You open up a passage to the child within.

And that child — I'm scared to say this, so I've got to — that child, to me, is God. They are one and the same.

When we were children, God was everywhere. Remember? We could smell him, roll around in him — or her, right? Everything was God. That rock the girl had the other day.

You understand where I'm getting my fear about talking about this. From childhood. We were told that people think you're weird if you talk about such things.

You can talk about co-dependency and depression, and mention masturbation, if you want to push your luck, but don't bring God into the conversation because they'll reach for the butterfly nets.

The only thing that cheers me up about growing old is that if you get old enough, you get to be like a child again. You don't care what people think. You wear what you want to because it's comfortable. You don't listen when people talk nonsense because you don't have to impress them — and life's at last really too short to do anything dumb! You sit smelling flowers or looking at rocks for hours.

I know an old woman like that, her memory going, and the nurse said, "She's almost reached nirvana."

She's moved back to where she was as a child. Back to herself before her parents and teachers and society remade her in their image. Back to God.

It's never too soon to begin that journey.

Well, I don't know how to finish this talk, because the thinking in it isn't done yet.

But it's nearly nine· — time to end. I said what I wanted to, and I'm very thankful to you for the good hearing you gave me.

Thanks!

We'll take a break, and then I'm going to enjoy hearing what you want to say.

After
Recovery

I said earlier that we don't get well right away and we don't get well completely.

We don't *recover.* We are always *recovering.* Or *in recovery.*

We don't recover because our illness is part of us, imprinted into our self. You can't "recover" from the fact that you're born male or female. Or in 1951 or 1940. Or blue-eyed or black-skinned or susceptible to chemical dependency. Or to this father and that mother.

You can't recover from your infancy and childhood. You can't recover from fate.

We all know this. "You can't change the past" — that's the way we usually put it.

Now in these talks I've been saying there is one thing about the past we *can* change. We can change the way we feel about it.

This is very important. It doesn't change the past, of course — it changes our relation to it. It opens up huge ranges of new life to adult children of dysfunctional families like you and me. It means we aren't locked into the false faces our parents put on us or the equally false faces we put on to rebel against them.

We can get free to be the selves we really are.

But getting free, getting better won't be the end of our problems. "After recovery" — in quotes — there's plenty of work to do.

First, and most important, we have to stay in recovery. Which means we have to continue the work that liberated us from our addictions. I've said a lot about this work in the talks you've already read, and my partner Bill Stott will tell you about his recovery work in a little while. So I'm not going to talk now about what you have to do to begin recovery.

Once you've begun recovery, you're going to find there are forces working against you. Your world is used to you being sick. It's not going to let you get well without a fight.

Because, you see, it isn't only you that's been sick — it's your world, too.

Now I've said that most co-dependents are afraid to work on their disease. They're afraid of therapy, afraid of treatment centers, afraid of workshops, afraid of support groups.

You know why they're afraid?

The main reason, I think — the hidden reason — is that they're afraid they might get better.

Weird, huh?

On some level they know that if they get better, they'll have to make some hard decisions about their life. Their spouse or lover, for example — do they really want to spend the rest of their lives with him or her? Do they really want to stop being mamma's baby or daddy's pride and joy? Do they really want to keep on at their demeaning job for that creep of a boss?

You get a little well and there are some kinds of shit you won't swallow.

A lot of us do awful work, in bad conditions, for terrible people. Most of us stay in denial about these things because otherwise we'd quit. We're ready to believe our Higher Power has better relationships in store for us, but we're not sure we can count on old H.P. for a better job.

Particularly these days in Austin.

I've seen a lot of people in recovery the last few years, and for most of them the work situation was the biggest hurdle — that or children. They get healthy. They break their addictions to chemicals and people. Then they go back to a sick work environment and feel themselves pulled down.

"I can't quit my job," they tell me. "I know it's sick, but I can't. My boss is a pig, and he's damaging my recovery and my soul, but I can't quit."

I've known some people in recovery who found they had to change their jobs. I know a corporate lawyer who switched to environmental law because he wanted to work at something he believed in. And I know another guy who gave up being a salesman, got his certification and is teaching school.

Most people stick to the same job, though. And that's fine. There's usually no reason to change. All honest work is honorable, and I suspect most of it can be made safe for human consumption too.

But when people say, "I know my job is bad for me — I just can't quit," I get worried, because it sounds like they may still be driven by fear and addiction. It sounds like Mom and Dad convinced the child's false self to be a lawyer or to make a lot of money or to have only dead-end jobs because the child was a disappointment, and the child still hasn't thrown off the old commands.

If you know something's bad for you, the thing to do is change it.

If it's your spouse who's bad for you, if your spouse's needs won't let you stay in recovery, you may have to divorce. There are some kinds of health that almost kill you.

There are a lot of books now that tell you how to change your spouse, your lover, your child, anybody you please. The books are cheats.

You can't change your spouse or child or anybody. Only *they* can do it. You can give them reasons to change. You can state clearly and without bitterness what you want and what you won't accept, but it's up to them to change.

If they don't, then it's up to you.

Being in recovery, you have already changed the ground rules of your relationships. You have changed the way you relate to other people. Formerly *they* were the center of your universe. Now *you* are — and that's got to rock the boat. Formerly you worked 55, 60 hours a week with no overtime.

Now you stop at 40, so you have time to care for yourself. Formerly they chose the movie, the night on the town, the summer vacation, and you tagged along whether you felt like it or not. Now you stay home and read a book. Formerly the husband was the lord of the manor. Now he's a slave like everybody else.

Which leads me gracefully to the issue of sex. Or gender, rather — sorry.

Some of you all aren't as antiquated as I am. I can remember seeing my mom serve everyone else their meals before eating herself, because that's what she was taught she was supposed to do. In some ways that gave her self-worth, self-esteem. By denying who she was and what her own wishes were, she believed she was a better person.

Our culture conditions women to subservience. My mom came from the South, where this view is especially strong. A woman was supposed to give her man what he needed when he needed it. Do her duty and not ask questions.

Most women today don't share that view. You women don't, right?

But you can't tell me that if your mom and dad were raised with that view, it didn't leave a mark on you. Because they modeled behavior for you — whether you copied what they did or rejected it.

Now I don't mean to accuse you all of benighted views. I'll talk about me, since I'm always the worst-case scenario.

I was raised, male, in the American South in the 1950s and 1960s, and I was taught — by my father *and* my mother, as well as by the other males and females in that society — that there were two kinds of second-class citizens: blacks and women. I was taught, as a well-brought-up boy, to pretend to respect both groups but *not really do it.*

(Audience comments.)

Listen, I'm telling you the truth here — *my* truth. *(Laughs)* I'm not saying you have to like it or agree with it.

The message I picked up about women was that they weren't as important as men. Their characters weren't as deep. Oh, there were some exceptions — saints and Emily Dickinson. But by and large, women could be used, abused, screwed and losed. And then you could get yourself another one.

Some things haven't changed much, eh?

You remember that high school riddle they played on you? They gave you a card that said something like "Men tear open my wrapper, squeeze me to their lips, crush me in corners, and throw me away. And how can I help myself when I'm only . . ." and you turned the card over and the answer was "a cigarette?" *(Audience laughs.)*

Pretty sick stuff, huh? Before you knew the answer you were embarrassed to the roots of your hair, thinking, "How can they say this in public about a woman?"

Because you knew it was true! Was what people — men and women — thought was true.

When you've grown up with those beliefs, as I did — grown up watching your father treat your mother far worse than he treated the plumber who came to fix the sink — is it any wonder you have problems with women? I mean, I'm lucky they even *talk* to me.

The feminists are right. We come from a sexist society. We've got to change the whole way we think.

Where the feminists are wrong — some of them, at least — is they devalue the roles that women traditionally have taken.

Teacher. Nurse. Mother.

There aren't any roles better than those.

I was thinking about this the other day when I was at the beach, watching a young mother tend her child. The child was a toddler, making pies in the sand. I wasn't sure whether it was a boy or a girl until later when her mother changed her diaper.

You could see right away the mother was bored. Having to fill the pail with sand and turn it over neatly so it was a perfect cylinder for her kid to knock down. "'Nother, Ma!" the child yelled, and the mother filled the pail again. She was bored having to pay attention to this fountain of energy she'd brought into the world.

And I remembered how when I was younger, I used to feel sorry for women who had to take care of babies while their husbands and I could go off to *important, interesting* work.

You know, like selling shoes and insurance. *(Audience laughs.)* Or, maybe worse, going to graduate school.

I really wanted to say to the woman, "There isn't any more important work than what you're doing. Someday you'll realize this — probably with regret. You're shaping a child's whole life."

Now, understand, I'm not saying that a *woman* has to do this work. A man can do it. Many men *are* doing it. I hope someday to have the privilege of doing it.

What I'm saying is that I strongly disagree with anyone — feminist or male chauvinist — who undervalues this work.

And I guess I'm saying something directly to the women in the audience: As you work toward becoming the person you really are, don't be swayed by other people's opinions of what "a woman" is. Or does. Or wants.

Don't listen to *shoulds* from anybody. The only person you have to please is yourself. That's hard enough work for one human.

Now maybe some of you are thinking, "John makes being in recovery sound so tough I think I'll stay sick."

Yeah. Well, it *is* tough, sad to say. It's tough for people like us who grew up in dysfunctional families. Because healthy behavior isn't normal for us. We have to remind ourselves to be healthy.

Because of the families we come from, recovery is a lifetime process we never get done with.

Growing up in addictive relationships, we learned to look to other people to fix us. We kept feeling that *someone else* or some one *thing* or *process* — a sports car, a new drug or diet or job or lover or guru — was going to make the world perfect for us.

I'm here to tell you no. Your world isn't going to be made right once and for all.

It's going to be better. Healthier. Saner. You're going to be happier than you've ever been. But it's not going to be a bed of roses.

I always loved the title of the book *I Never Promised You A Rose Garden*. That's what I'm promising you: no rose garden.

Life isn't *hard*, as our parents said it was. But it isn't perfect either.

When you've worked through the fears behind your co-dependency and given up living by your old patterns, often your secondary addictions drop away. You don't need coffee and cigarettes and alcohol so much. You can give up caffeine and not have headaches, give up nicotine and alcohol and not get the shakes. Because you will have dealt with the causes of your need.

But recovery is tricky — you've got to be careful. I've seen it happen many times, and I've read about it, that people in recovery relapse because they feel abandoned.

I was working with a client the other day, and we went deeper into his pain than ever before. All the feeling he had been repressing came out — crying, anger, sadness. He was important enough in his company to where he could have taken the rest of the day off, as I suggested. He didn't do it because, being co-dependent, he worried about what people in his office would think.

Back at work, feelings from the session kept coming up, and he had to swallow them. He didn't get anything done. Then, as he was driving home, lo and behold, though he's not much of a drinker, he stopped at a bar for a quick one. Five Margaritas later, they had to call him a taxi.

He spoke to me the next day. He couldn't understand what had happened.

"I felt good after the session," he said, "but I felt empty."

Those of you who have worked with me or done emotional release work with other therapists know what he was talking about. After the work, you feel good, but you feel cleared out. Kind of empty.

Well, in this culture, what we're taught is, when you're empty, get stuffed. Put something in that emptiness, quick. Alcohol. Valium. Aspirin. Food. Work. TV. Sex.

Your woman leaves, find another.

You've seen the bumper sticker: "When the going gets tough, the tough go shopping." The malls of America are full of junkies, I'm not kidding.

Tammy Faye Bakker — did you notice this? — Tammy Faye said her hobby is shopping. If the spirit of Jesus leaves you, try Sears. Sears has everything.

Emptiness is the enemy.

Now this isn't the way the Easterners think. If you read their religious literature, it's all the time talking about empty jars, empty vases, empty windows, empty rooms. Emptiness is the norm for them — nothing to be afraid of.

Being in recovery is living fearlessly with emptiness. Knowing that emptiness is healthy. Knowing that your real self grows out of emptiness. Knowing that as you get well you are forced more and more into yourself and your emptiness.

Which leads me to my last point, and my saddest.

I've found that being in recovery means I have fewer friends and many, *many* fewer dates. *(Audience laughs.)*

It's true. Used to be, I had lots of dates because I needed to fill my emptiness. I'd date *anybody!* No discretion whatsoever. All ages, all IQs, all interests — only please make sure they're damaged. You know, so I can go into my rescuing routine.

Now I don't do it. I see people's neediness. I think, "I just don't want to take that on. My system isn't up to it anymore."

Is this because I do counseling? I don't think so.

I think I'm getting better. I'm not willing to bear other people's burdens, as you have to if you're in a relationship with a co-dependent. I'm tired of setting my boundaries, saying healthy things like, "Sweetheart, that's your problem. I don't want to get involved," and being chewed out for it because the woman thinks I'm as cruel as an ax murderer.

As I say, in recovery you get more and more forced on yourself. You have your friends, and they're wonderful but fewer in number. You don't have your 99th soulmate — which is fine because you don't believe in soulmates anymore. You don't even have somebody you want to take to the Saturday movie.

But you feel fine. You are healthy and happy alone.

Because you have yourself. And you have to feel that's enough. That's just as it should be.

That's life — *your* life.

Well, thank you very much for your attention during all these talks, those of you who've come for the whole series. And thanks to those of you who just came tonight. I hope many of you will be able to make the workshop tomorrow, because we're going to put some of the things I've been talking about into practice. Specifically, getting in touch with your feelings.

Those of you who haven't been to a workshop before, I don't want you to be worried. I promise it will be very safe and healing. Very comfortable. That's why I ask you to bring a pillow and a towel — you know, something you can hug and something you can cry into. *(Audience laughs.)*

Those of you who can't make the workshop, don't worry. You're recovering like the rest of us, at just the right rate for you.

None of us needs fixing because none of us is broken. That's what we've got to learn and feel.

If I don't see you tomorrow, I'll see you again soon, I hope. Take good care of yourself.

Another Note From Bill Stott

We had some pages left to fill and John said, "Why don't
you do it? You've been all through this" — *this* being the pain
of becoming an independent person. "You came out okay. Tell
us how."

I said I couldn't do that because it would repeat too much
of what he had already said in the book.

"Say things I haven't said," John said.

"Yeah, ha, ha, be original," I said.

"Everyone's original," he said.

John sometimes says things that make it hard to argue
with him.

I said, "Maybe you won't agree with what I say."

"Bill, I'll tell you what. You rewrote what I said till you
agreed with it. I'll do the same."

"Well . . . okay."

A word of introduction first.

In my mid-40s, the shameful demon that had pursued me
from my youth — the memory of a woman I had loved and
lost — took such hold of my mind that life became bitter and
empty for me. After much suffering I learned that my problem

wasn't the demon, as I had always thought, but my compulsive, co-dependent childhood, which had taught me shame.

I owe this realization to John. At his suggestion, I grieved and raged and broke free of the good little boy in the box my parents made me. Having done so now, I no longer feel cheated of my life. I am happier than I ever thought I'd be.

In my recovery I was helped by many of the suggestions John makes in this book. I was helped also by suggestions and realizations that came from other friends, from books and — sometimes — from what felt like the truest part of myself. I list the suggestions and realizations in the order in which they came to me, so far as I recall it.

• See a doctor. If you are depressed — certainly if you have recurrent thoughts of suicide, as I did — the first step toward recovery is acknowledging your illness and seeking help. Your doctor is likely to send you to a psychiatrist, who will determine whether your problem is biological and needs to be treated with drugs. If not, if you are just a normal neurotic like John and me, the psychiatrist is likely to recommend counseling with a psychotherapist.

• Do psychotherapy. It costs a lot of money, but it will teach you a lot and change your life. Choose a psychotherapist you like as a person, who may not be the first one you interview. Try a psychotherapist for a session or two, and if you don't feel rapport, try another. If that one isn't right either, try a third. A fourth. A fifth. Don't worry that you will hurt a psychotherapist's feelings if you choose not to work with him or her, or when you decide to stop consulting. The psychotherapist is your employee, there to help you.

• Don't be ashamed of your suffering. Don't be proud of it, but don't be ashamed. And don't be frightened. Everybody suffers: It's part of the human condition, like picking your nose.

• Tell the truth about your suffering to anyone who won't be badly hurt by the truth. Shame has kept you silent; the only way to overcome shame is to speak up.

• Attend 12-Step meetings: Alcoholics Anonymous, Adult Children of Alcoholics, Al-Anon, Co-Dependents Anonymous, Gamblers Anonymous, Overeaters Anonymous, Narcotics

Anonymous, Sex and Love Addicts Anonymous (sometimes referred to as the Augustine Fellowship) and so on. It is a great help to hear other people working to break their patterns of compulsive feeling and behavior.

• Learn yoga breathing (don't be put off by the word *yoga*). Breathe in and out through your nose slowly and deeply, counting to four as you inhale, counting to two as you hold your breath, counting to four as you exhale. Many people find it helps to close their eyes as they breathe. Such breathing will calm you. If, like me, you get stress pains in your gut, it will ease them. You don't have to do yoga breathing for long. I do a dozen breaths at a time, maximum, and no more than 30 in a day. They are relaxation, not work.

• Have a few friends you tell *everything* to. (John is such a friend for me and I for him.) Some people use themselves as their confidant, talking out their problems in a journal or internal conversations. I like being able to talk or write to someone outside myself.

• Don't hesitate to hate your parents whenever that feeling comes up. If you feel better not seeing them, don't see them. Anything you owe them you paid back long ago.

• Don't hesitate to hate anyone who has hurt you. There is nothing wrong with feeling whatever you feel.

• If there are things you have fervently wanted to do but forbidden yourself — like having an affair, scuba diving, gaining ten pounds — do them unless they are really dangerous. The psychologist B.F. Skinner says the object of life is to gratify yourself without getting arrested.

• As you let yourself be freer in your life, you'll find you need to let the people close to you be freer in theirs. Otherwise, you'll be a captive to controlling them. I found I had to let my wife spend a fair portion of the money I'd been having us save.

• Spend time in nature. If you are sad, say to yourself as you walk, "I belong here on the earth. I belong here as much as anyone."

• Dance — it helps put you back into your body. When I'm in front of a mirror, I try to remember to do some rumba twists with my belly. When I was feeling angry a lot of the

time, I shadowboxed. I could be as violent as I liked and no
one was hurt.

• Scream. Howl. Shriek. Bellow. I do it when I'm driving
the car and feel oppressed. I keep the windows rolled up.
When I'm stopped at a light, I shut up. Or I laugh.

• Laugh. At everything that goes right or wrong for you.
When I started getting better, I found I had a different laugh
than before: deeper, longer, smoother.

• Cry. Whenever you can and as much as you can. After
crying I feel not only calmer but more content. I cry almost
every day, usually at things I read in the paper or hear on *All
Things Considered.*

• Sing. Singing also puts you back in your body.

• Read books that make you feel better — self-help books
like this. Books that talk about getting well will give you ideas
you can use in your life because, just as everyone's sufferings
are like everyone else's, so are our ways of getting well.

• Have lots of ways of pulling yourself out of a down time.
Funnily enough, this idea occurred to me long after I had
started collecting ways.

• Always pay attention to your pain. My psychotherapist,
Faith Starnes, a Bioenergetics and addiction specialist, made
me realize this. I had been taught to discount my pain, indeed
to be proud of acting as though it didn't exist. Wrong! John
and Faith are right: Your body is the sure barometer of your
mental state. As I suggested earlier, pain for me comes in the
gut (I have a spastic colon). It starts as a slight heaviness and
never gets worse than a dull ache. Whenever I can feel my gut,
I know I am in a false position (a co-dependent pattern, John
would say) and have to do something to change.

• Realize — *really* realize — that nobody is responsible for
your current unhappiness but you. If you're not happy, that's
your problem. If you won't act to make yourself feel better,
you're a fool.

• Realize — *really* realize — that you are not responsible
for anyone else's happiness, except your children's when they
are very young. If the people in your life aren't happy, that's
their problem.

• Realize — *really* realize — that you don't have to live up to any ideal, even your own.

• Talk down the negative voice in your head telling you that you're going to fail at what you do, that you're no good, that you're making a mess of your life and the lives of others. Two books that suggest how to do this are Susan Jeffers' *Feel the Fear: And Do It Anyway* and David D. Burns' *Feeling Good: The New Mood Therapy.*

• When I'm blue, I sometimes find myself thinking of painful times in my childhood. I find it comforting to imagine myself as I am now comforting myself as I was then — timid, unnaturally serious. I put my arm around the boy, give him a kiss on the forehead, and say things like, "Billy, everything's going to be fine. I'm going to take care of you. You're never going to be alone again. Your parents didn't give you the attention you needed, but I'm going to. You can count on me to be there. Always. Nothing's going to harm you."

• When I think of painful times in my adulthood, I talk to myself as I was then, saying things like, "Bill, don't worry about it. You did the best you could. You thought you were doing the right thing. And you learned from the experience. You wouldn't do it again — which proves you learned. Don't punish yourself. People do dumb, unlucky things sometimes. You have a perfect right to be wrong." In my healthiest moods I feel I had to make the mistakes I made in the past to be as happy as I am now.

• When I'm wondering what to do, I sometimes think "What would a happy, well-loved child do?" and then I do it. I say off-the-wall things that puzzle or amuse those about me. I start singing in unlikely places. I go to bed two hours early.

• When I'm doing something disagreeable or boring, I remember Jung's words: "The great thing is here and now — this is the eternal moment. And if you do not realize it, you have missed the best part of your life."

• You have to be able to walk away from any relationship, no matter how much you love the other person. You have to be able to say to the other person, though you may not have to *actually* say it: "I don't need to love you. I don't need to make love to you. I don't need you to love me. I don't need

to please you. I don't need you." As a child, you had to love
your mother and father. As a 15- or 20- or 25-year-old, you had
to have someone love you to prove you were lovable. Now
you're an adult. You're free. You can be yourself.

• You have to live most of your life with yourself: Rejoice in
that fact. Don't expect anyone to interest you day in, day out
— they won't. Don't count on being intimate with someone
else all the time — intimacy comes and goes. There are no
final fixes.

• Read the mystics. They put our life in perspective. Here's
Rumi, the 13th century Sufi poet:

> Take someone who doesn't keep' score,
> who's not looking to be richer, or afraid of losing,
> who has not the slightest interest even
> in his own personality: he's free.

Here's Lao Tsu, the founder of Taoism:

> The pursuit of power accumulates things;
> The Right Way discards them.
> Do less and less until you're doing nothing:
> When you're doing nothing, nothing is undone.
> You rule the world by letting it happen.
> You can't rule it by interfering.

And he again:

> Give up seeking command and perfection,
> And things will be much better.

• In short: Let go of whatever you can't control. Which is
almost everything.

Cassette Tape Series

. . . is available from John Lee at Austin Men's Center, 1611 West Sixth St., Austin, TX 78703. Phone: (512) 477-9595. In a powerful and often humorous way, these tapes help you make sense out of the emotional confusion caused by growing up in an alcoholic or dysfunctional family. They also help men better understand themselves and help women understand men.

- Why Men Can't Feel And The Price Women Pay
- Expressing Your Anger Appropriately
- Grieving; A Key To Healing
- Healing The Father-Son Wound
- What Co-dependency Really Is
- Addictive Relationships
- Saying Goodbye To Mom And Dad
- Couples, Caring And Co-dependency
- The Flying Boy: Healing the Wounded Man Workshop*
  *3 tapes at $24.95 plus $2.50 for postage & handling. All other tapes are $9.95 each plus $1.95 for postage and handling. Texas residents add 8% sales tax.

New Tapes From John Lee

- What's Going On With Men: Intimacy, Feelings & Relationships
- Dating, Loving & Living With The Adult Child
- Finding Our Fathers, Finding Our Feelings

To schedule John Lee for a lecture or workshop, contact Allen Maurer at New Men's Press.

Austin Men's Center

A Safe Place for Men, Women and Children

Executive Director: John Lee

We of the Austin Men's Center integrate psychological, physical and spiritual approaches to growth, change and recovery. A holistic philosophy is used in the care and treatment of individuals who engage in the center's services. The staff, including both men and women, work with men, women and children because the issues of one's sex and age cannot be dealt with in isolation.

Specializations include: Men's Issues and Masculine Psychology, Addictive Relationships and Addictions in general, Co-dependency, Adult Children from Dysfunctional Families and Incest Survivors.

We use a combination of counseling, Gestalt, bioenergetics, Jungian, deep tissue body work (including Rolfing, Shiatsu and Trager massage), dream work, nutritional counseling, martial arts and yoga.

The Center is a focal point for ongoing support groups and information on the Men's Movement and Adult Children work around the country.

Austin Men's Center is also the home of the Primary Emotional Energy Recovery (PEER) Training Program. This training is for counselors and therapists who want to more fully bring the body and the emotions back into the recovery process. The PEER program, an excellent system for accessing and discharging grief and anger, is conducted by John Lee, Dan Jones (Ph.D.) and staff.

For more information write to Austin Men's Center, 1611 West Sixth St., Austin, TX 78703. Phone: (512) 477-9595.

Notes

Notes

Other Books Available by John Lee

I DON'T WANT TO BE ALONE
For Men And Women Who Want To Heal
Addictive Relationships

Most people want a relationship with someone special — but at what price? Would you stay in a relationship in which you are unhappy? Would the fear of being alone keep you from leaving?

Lee describes such a relationship and his realization that he is staying in the relationship because of his fear of being alone.

If you are in a relationship that doesn't make you happy, ask yourself, "Why?" Then read *I Don't Want To Be Alone* — you'll be glad you did.

ISBN 1-55874-065-1   (Soft cover 5½ x 8½   pp. 140)
Code 0651 .... $8.95
Also available in audio cassette

THE FLYING BOY:
Healing The Wounded Man

This book is a record of one man's journey to find his "true masculinity," and his way out of co-dependent and addictive relation-

ships. It is for all men and women who grew up in dysfunctional families and are now ready for some fresh insights into their past and their pain. *The Flying Boy* opens doors to understanding for both men and women.

ISBN 1-55874-006-6
(Soft cover 5½ x 8½   128 pp.)
Code 0066 .... $7.95
Also available in audio cassette

Available from
Health Communications, Inc.
Deerfield Beach, Florida

Books from . . .
Health Communications

Other Books By . . .
Health Communications

ADULT CHILDREN OF ALCOHOLICS
Janet Woititz
Over a year on *The New York Times* Best-Seller list, this book is the primer on Adult Children of Alcoholics.
ISBN 0-932194-15-X   **$6.95**

STRUGGLE FOR INTIMACY
Janet Woititz
Another best-seller, this book gives insightful advice on learning to love more fully.
ISBN 0-932194-25-7   **$6.95**

BRADSHAW ON: THE FAMILY: A Revolutionary Way of Self-Discovery
John Bradshaw
The host of the nationally televised series of the same name shows us how families can be healed and individuals can realize full potential.
ISBN 0-932194-54-0   **$9.95**

HEALING THE SHAME THAT BINDS YOU
John Bradshaw
This important book shows how toxic shame is the core problem in our compulsions and offers new techniques of recovery vital to all of us.
ISBN 0-932194-86-9   **$9.95**

HEALING THE CHILD WITHIN: Discovery and Recovery for
Adult Children of Dysfunctional Families — Charles Whitfield, M.D.
Dr. Whitfield defines, describes and discovers how we can reach our Child Within to heal and nurture our woundedness.
ISBN 0-932194-40-0   **$8.95**

A GIFT TO MYSELF: A Personal Guide To Healing My Child Within
Charles L. Whitfield, M.D.
Dr. Whitfield provides practical guidelines and methods to work through the pain and confusion of being an Adult Child of a dysfunctional family.
ISBN 1-55874-042-2   **$11.95**

HEALING TOGETHER: A Guide To Intimacy And Recovery For
Co-dependent Couples — Wayne Kritsberg, M.A.
This is a practical book that tells the reader why he or she gets into dysfunctional and painful relationships, and then gives a concrete course of action on how to move the relationship toward health.
ISBN 1-55784-053-8   **$8.95**

3201 S.W. 15th Street,
Deerfield Beach, FL 33442
1-800-851-9100

Health
Communications, Inc.

Helpful 12-Step Books from . . .
Health Communications

12 STEPS TO SELF-PARENTING For Adult Children
Philip Oliver-Diaz, M.S.W., and Patricia A. O'Gorman, Ph.D.

This gentle 12-Step guide takes the reader from pain to healing and self-parenting, from anger to forgiveness, and from fear and despair to recovery.

ISBN 0-932194-68-0 $7.95

SELF-PARENTING 12-STEP WORKBOOK: Windows To Your Inner Child
Patricia O'Gorman, Ph.D., and Philip Oliver-Diaz, M.S.W.

This workbook invites you to become the complete individual you were born to be by using visualizations, exercises and experiences designed to reconnect you to your inner child.

ISBN 1-55874-052-X $9.95

THE 12-STEP STORY BOOKLETS
Mary M. McKee

Each beautifully illustrated booklet deals with a step, using a story from nature in parable form. The 12 booklets (one for each step) lead us to a better understanding of ourselves and our recovery.

ISBN 1-55874-002-3 $8.95

VIOLENT VOICES:
12 Steps To Freedom From Emotional And Verbal Abuse
Kay Porterfield, M.A.

By using the healing model of the 12 Steps emotionally abused women are shown how to deal effectively with verbal and psychological abuse and to begin living as healed and whole people.

ISBN 1-55874-028-7 $9.95

GIFTS FOR PERSONAL GROWTH & RECOVERY
Wayne Kritsberg

A goldmine of positive techniques for recovery (affirmations, journal writing, visualizations, guided meditations, etc.), this book is indispensable for those seeking personal growth.

ISBN 0-932194-60-5 $6.95

3201 S.W. 15th Street,
Deerfield Beach, FL 33442
1-800-851-9100

Health Communications, Inc.